A BRUSH WITH SHAKESPEARE
THE BARD IN PAINTING, 1780-1910

COVER: **Wladyslaw Von Czachorski**
Polish, 1850-1911
The Actors Before Hamlet, 1875 (detail)
Cat. No. 13

Editor: Ross Anderson
Designer: Jane Thomas
Copy Editor: Wanda O'Shello
Type: Goudy Old Style
Typesetting: Compos-it, Inc.
Printing: Moran Colorgraphic

This exhibition, conceived in celebration of the premiere season of the Alabama Shakespeare Festival in Montgomery, was organized by Ross Anderson, Director of the Montgomery Museum of Fine Arts.

This exhibition and accompanying catalogue were made possible by generous grants from the City of Montgomery, Montgomery County, the Montgomery Museum of Fine Arts Association, and the Alabama State Council on the Arts and Humanities.

·A BRUSH WITH· ·SHAKESPEARE·
· THE BARD IN PAINTING: 1780~1910 ·

Montgomery Museum of Fine Arts
Montgomery, Alabama

Exhibition Schedule

Montgomery Museum of Fine Arts, *Montgomery, Alabama*
December 11, 1985 through February 2, 1986

The New York Public Library at Lincoln Center,
The Library and the Museum of the Performing Arts, *New York, New York*
March 10 through April 13, 1986

The Chicago Public Library Cultural Center, *Chicago, Illinois*
April 26 through June 14, 1986

Copyright 1985 by the Montgomery Museum of Fine Arts.
All rights reserved. No portion of this book may be reproduced without the written permission of the Montgomery Museum of Fine Arts, 440 South McDonough Street, Montgomery, Alabama 36104 (205) 832-2976

Library of Congress Cataloging-in-Publication Data
Main entry under title:

A Brush with Shakespeare.

  Bibliography: p.
  1. Shakespeare, William, 1564-1616—Illustrations—Exhibitions. 2. Painting, English—Exhibitions.
3. Painting, American—Exhibitions. 4. Painting, Modern—17th-18th centuries—England—Exhibitions.
5. Painting, Modern—17th-18th centuries—United States—Exhibitions. 6. Painting, Modern 19th century—England—Exhibitions. 7. Painting, Modern—19th century—United States—Exhibitions. 8. Shakespeare, William, 1564-1616—Stage history—1800-1950—Addresses, essays, lectures. I. Montgomery Museum of Fine Arts.
PR2883.B78   1985   822.3′3   85-29669

ISBN 0-89280-024-0

TABLE OF CONTENTS

Foreword 1
"Words into Pictures: Shakespeare in British Art, 1760-1900" 3
"Shakespeare and the Theatre of Illustration" 23
Catalogue of the Exhibition 35
Bibliography 93

LENDERS TO THE EXHIBITION

The Ackland Art Museum
The University of North Carolina at Chapel Hill
Chapel Hill, North Carolina

The Boston Athenaeum
Boston, Massachusetts

Carlisle Museum and Art Gallery
Carlisle, England

Carnegie Institute, Museum of Art
Pittsburgh, Pennsylvania

The Corcoran Gallery of Art
Washington, D.C.

Mr. and Mrs. E. Hal Dickson, Mr. and Mrs. James R. Duncan and Mr. and Mrs. Frank W. Rose
San Angelo, Texas

The Folger Shakespeare Library
Washington, D.C.

The FORBES Magazine Collection
New York, New York

Garrick Club
London, England

The Walter Hampden-Edwin Booth Theater Collection and Library at The Players
New York, New York

Bob Jones University Art Gallery and Museum
Greenville, South Carolina

Leighton House Museum and Art Gallery
London, England

The Honorable Francis D. Murnaghan, Jr.
Baltimore, Maryland

Peter Nahum
London, England

The National Portrait Gallery
Washington, D.C.

National Theatre of Great Britain
London, England

New Orleans Museum of Art
New Orleans, Louisiana

The Pennsylvania Academy of the Fine Arts
Philadelphia, Pennsylvania

Museo de Arte de Ponce
Ponce, Puerto Rico

Royal Academy of Arts
London, England

Smith College Museum of Art
Northampton, Massachusetts

University of Virginia Art Museum
Charlottesville, Virginia

Vassar College Art Gallery
Poughkeepsie, New York

Wadsworth Atheneum
Hartford, Connecticut

Yale University Art Gallery
New Haven, Connecticut

Foreword

This exhibition and accompanying catalogue explore the use of plays by William Shakespeare as subject matter for painters in the late 18th and 19th centuries, when such a theme was at its peak of popularity in England, America, and continental Europe. It was conceived to help celebrate the opening of the impressive new facilities for the Alabama Shakespeare Festival in Montgomery; we offer it as a salute from the city's oldest cultural institution to its newest and certainly its most ambitious sister organization. Operating for fourteen years during the summer months in a high school auditorium in Anniston, Alabama, the Festival's new home in Montgomery will be a stunning two-theatre complex; in its initial season, forty professional actors will perform ten plays in repertory over a forty-week period. We at the Museum wish the Festival every success in its monumental new endeavor; it is with keen anticipation that we contemplate forthcoming dramatic productions, and we look forward to the Festival being a source of entertainment and education of the highest quality for audiences from central Alabama and surrounding regions for generations to come.

Aside from its Shakespeare theme, this exhibition is additionally appropriate to commemorate the opening of the Festival in that it confronts issues concerning the relationship of different art forms. Too often, we feel, we tend to appreciate paintings or plays or books only in relation to works of a similar nature; victims in our formative years of strictly defined academic departments, perhaps, we are asked not only to subdivide our critical faculties when considering various art forms, but often to declare loyalties as well, and to dismiss as impure works of art that engage more than one of our senses at a time. Painters represented in this exhibition felt emphatically otherwise. As the following essays lucidly establish, while these artists may have felt great respect for Shakespeare's genius, their regard did not inhibit them from freely adapting the Bard's words into visual images, nor were they shy about adding to, subtracting from, or altering drastically elements in the playwright's text to suit their own aesthetic predilections. Whether Shakespeare's achievement is enriched or degraded by the transformation is for the viewer of the exhibition to decide.

As for us, we favor vigorous interaction among the arts, and that is fortunate, for we are in an enviable position to promote our views. When planning for this exhibition was first begun, the Museum's attitude toward the Shakespeare Festival was one of simple admiration and encouragement. Presently, however, we will find ourselves in a more intimate relation: several weeks ago the decision was made to locate our own new facility to property adjoining the Shakespeare site. When the new Museum opens in 1987, it will be our pleasure to walk from our galleries out to a terrace, where from across a pond and gently rolling terrain we will view the superb proportions of the Festival building. This proximity, aside from serving the practical goals of mutual promotion and shared audiences, will also encourage cooperation of an aesthetic kind: exhibitions and seminars devoted to costume and set design, perhaps; presentations of performance art; *son et lumière* extravaganzas on the generous expanses of Wynfield Park. The possibilities excite us tremendously, and we look forward to a long and fruitful relationship between the two institutions.

We owe a debt of gratitude to many who helped make this exhibition a success. I thank first our contributors to the catalogue: Lucy Oakley, Research Assistant, Metropolitan Museum of Art; Cary Mazer, Assistant Professor, University of Pennsylvania, and Margaret Lynn Ausfeld, our own Acting Curator. Additional staff members who were especially helpful include David Gilbert, Assistant Director for Curatorial Affairs; Pamela Bransford, Registrar; Jodi Bolling, Secretary; Patrick Kirkland, Preparator; and Ami Simpson, Publicity Coordinator. For their efforts in printing the catalogue I thank also Jane Thomas, Wanda O'Shello and Margaret Carpenter. We are grateful for the generous cooperation of all our lenders, but particularly to Messrs. Dickson, Rose, and Duncan of San Angelo, Texas, whose substantial collection of Shakespearean works make up such a significant portion of our show. For their help in facilitating loans, I wish to thank especially Sir Hugh Casson, Director Emeritus, The Royal Academy of Arts; Phillip Knachel, Associate Director, The Folger Shakespeare Library; and Kurt Schon and his staff, Kurt Schon, Ltd.

For their cooperation in helping to orchestrate the exhibition tour, I thank Edmée Slocum and Patricia Barton of the Shakespeare Globe Center; Dr. Robert Henderson, Chief, General Library and Museum of the Performing Arts, the New York Public Library; and Gregory Knight, Chief Curator, the Chicago Public Library Cultural Center.

For continuing support of Museum operations and funding for this exhibition, we owe a debt of gratitude to the City of Montgomery and Mayor Emory Folmar, whose advocacy of the arts in our city is truly extraordinary. Also generously contributing to our efforts is the Montgomery County Commission, Joel Barfoot, Chairman, and the Alabama State Council on the Arts and Humanities, Albert Head, Executive Director. Indispensible aid was also provided by the Montgomery Museum of Fine Arts Association under the leadership of James Scott, President; to him and his hard working Board of Trustees, we offer sincere thanks.

I close with a note of appreciation to Winton M. Blount. It was he and his wife Carolyn who donated as a gift to Montgomery the magnificent building that houses the Alabama Shakespeare Festival, thereby instigating a statewide fund-raising effort that will result in our city being the home of the finest, most extensive performing arts complex in the Southeast. But his generosity does not stop there. When the new Museum opens in 1987, it will stand on land donated by Mr. Blount, and will have as the nucleus of its permanent collection forty-one important paintings by American artists of the first rank, a magnificent gift from the corporate collection of Blount, Inc. Red, what can we say? We thank you; we really do.

Ross Anderson
Director
Montgomery Museum of Fine Arts

Words into Pictures: Shakespeare in British Art, 1760-1900

By Lucy Oakley

From the early 1760s, when Shakespeare was first canonized as England's greatest dramatist, a controversy has raged between those who insist that the purest experience of his meaning is to be had in reading his written words, and those who believe that the fullest potential of the plays can only be realized in the dramatic arts.[1] The Romantic essayist Charles Lamb spoke for the first group when he denounced as insidious the pleasures and satisfactions produced by a fine Shakespearean performance. Of his first experience in seeing one of Shakespeare's tragedies on stage, with the great actors John Philip Kemble and his sister Sarah Siddons in the leading roles, he wrote:

> *It seemed to embody and realize conceptions which had hitherto assumed no distinct shape. But dearly do we pay all our life after for this juvenile pleasure, this sense of distinctness. When the novelty is past, we find to our cost that instead of realizing an idea, we have only materialized and brought down a fine vision to the standard of flesh and blood. We have let go a dream, in quest of an unattainable substance.*[2]

Lamb condemned pictorial as well as dramatic realizations of Shakespeare's plays: "I am jealous of the combination of the sister arts. Let them sparkle apart. What injury (short of the theatres) did not Boydell's 'Shakespeare Gallery' do me with Shakespeare . . . To be tied down to an authentic face of Juliet. To have Imogen's portrait! to confine the illimitable!"[3]

For Lamb and like-minded partisans, the essence of Shakespeare's genius lay in his sacred text, unsullied by the intermediary of actor or artist. For the rival camp, however, the true significance of Shakespeare's plays can be captured only in the living tradition of the stage, or in the creative reinterpretation of the visual arts: Actors and artists literally resurrect the Elizabethan dramatist's message for contemporary audiences. "Surely the end of all plays is to be acted, and not to be simply read in the study," wrote Henry Irving, the leading actor-manager of the late Victorian stage. "Indeed there is no reason why we should praise [Shakespeare] as a dramatist if his plays will not bear acting," Irving continued, concluding: "The stage cannot be dissociated from Shakespeare, either as the poet or the man. It was the lever with which he moved the world; and, while we accord to him the supremacy of literature, it is but just to remember the practical aid he derived from his judgment and experience as a playwright and player."[4]

Like stage productions, works of art are vital components in the continuing saga of Shakespeare interpretation for, as W. Moelwyn Merchant has written, "every painting or engraving based on a poem or play is a critical gesture towards it source, a critical gesture the more potent in that it does not cease to be an original creative act."[5] As an act of translation from word into picture, Shakespearean art often tells the modern viewer as much about the manners and customs of the period in which it was produced as it sheds light on Shakespeare's meaning.

Shakespeare's profound insight into human nature, expressed with great variety in his many genres, periods, settings, and characters, ensured his attraction to a wide spectrum of painters and illustrators during the late eighteenth and nineteenth centuries, the heyday of literary and historical painting. Nearly 1400 Shakespearean subjects were shown at the Royal Academy in London from its first exhibition in 1769 until 1900, and more appeared at the smaller London and provincial societies and galleries.[6] Shakespeare's plays were performed regularly on stage during these years, and most Shakespearean paintings are tied in some way to the theatre. Some are outright portraits of famous actors in their Shakespearean roles. Others are connected less obviously with specific productions, but borrow from the stage in the selection of a particular scene for emphasis, in the interpretation of a character, in stage business, costume, or setting. The aesthetic concepts of an age, its theories of expression, were often shared by actors and artists. Theatrical presentations of Shakespeare's plays were frequently influenced by the previous visualizations of painters and illustrators, and stage productions were affected more directly by artists working as set and costume designers.

Prior to 1770, most representations of Shakespearean themes served utilitarian functions: they were frontispieces for editions of the plays or portraits of actors.[7] General interest in Shakespeare's plays increased sharply during the 1760s, stimulated by new editions and new criticism,[8] by the triumphant culmination of the career of the great Shakespearean actor David Garrick, and by the appearance of Shakespearean paintings at the first regular public art exhibitions. As Esther Dotson has noted, friendships among critics, artists, and actors become increasingly common at this time, just as the focus of their interest was shifting from the study of logic and reason to that of imagination and the passions.[9] Naturally they were attracted to Shakespeare's plays, the tragedies in particular, where the characters' innermost hopes, desires, dreams, and ambitions are laid bare.

The climax in the rediscovery of Shakespeare in the 1760s was the Shakespeare Jubilee, presented by David

Garrick at Stratford-upon-Avon in the last year of the decade. None of the plays were performed, but Shakespeare and his works were the focus of a three-day presentation of songs and pageants, with a final oration by Garrick himself. The festival attracted tremendous popular attention throughout England, and Garrick adapted some of the songs, the procession, and the crowning of Shakespeare's statue, which had been rained out at Stratford, as an afterpiece for the Drury Lane Theatre in London, where it enjoyed the longest run of the century.[10]

1. William Hogarth
David Garrick as Richard III, about 1745
Oil on canvas, 75 x 98½ in., Walker Art Gallery, Liverpool

Garrick was the preeminent Shakespeare actor of the mid-eighteenth century. For the highly conventionalized, stentorian delivery of his predecessors, he substituted a vivid, naturalistic acting style, one that played more directly on the audience's emotions. He created a sensation at his formal debut on the London stage as Richard III in 1741, and four years later sat for the famous portrait by William Hogarth (fig. 1), which departs from the conventional standing pose to capture the actor's innovative use of gesture and expression in conveying Richard's fright upon awakening from his troubled dream. Garrick was a master of self-promotion, and commissioned many of the more than 175 known portraits of himself; he was probably the most painted man in England in the eighteenth century.[11] He was acutely aware of the publicity value of showing his portraits at public exhibitions and distributing them widely through engravings and replicas. A close friend of many artists, including Hogarth, Francis Hayman, Johann Zoffany, Joshua Reynolds, and Benjamin West, Garrick was also a discerning collector and patron of wide-ranging tastes.

In 1768 the Royal Academy was founded, with Joshua Reynolds as its president. In a series of discourses delivered to the Academy's students from 1769 to 1790, Reynolds called upon his fellow artists to raise the level of English painting, hitherto confined mostly to portraiture, by rendering subjects from mythology, history, and literature

2. Nathaniel Dance
Timon of Athens, 1767
Oil on canvas, 48 x 54 in., Royal Collection, Great Britain

according to the technical and compositional principles of the great masters.[12] Reynolds' call for "grand manner" history painting was not new, but his *Discourses* were read widely and tremendously influential. British artists had long aspired to paint subjects more elevated than the portraits with which they earned their bread. The depiction of dramatic incidents from Shakespeare conformed easily to Reynolds' guidelines. An early example is Nathaniel Dance's *Timon of Athens* (fig. 2), exhibited at the Society of Artists in 1767, the year following the artist's return from eleven years of study in Rome, and purchased by George III. With its Greek subject, deliberately chosen to combine Shakespeare with classical antiquity, and its static, friezelike composition and marmoreal technique, derived from Poussin and antique sculpture, Dance's *Timon* is practically a Neoclassical manifesto. Just a few months after the opening of the Society's exhibition, the play, seldom performed during the eighteenth century, was revived by Dance's older brother, the actor James Love.[13] Dance subsequently found little patronage for history paintings, however, and turned almost exclusively to portraiture. His portrait of Garrick in the battle scene from Richard III (cat. no. 15), the original version of which was exhibited at the Royal Academy in 1771, stands squarely within the tradition of the actor portrait; the details of Garrick's sumptuous costume are emphasized, and the setting retains its character as a theatrical backcloth.

Neoclassic principles were not the only ones guiding painters of Shakespearean subjects in the 1760s. In 1767 John Runciman, a young Scottish artist working in Rome, painted a proto-Romantic *Lear in the Storm* (fig. 3), in which Lear's anguish is reflected and intensified in the raging tempest that sweeps up all of nature with its protean energy.[14] Runciman restored Shakespeare's Fool, who had been excised as an offense to propriety in the adaptation by Nahum Tate that had held the stage since 1681. Tate also had created a romance between Edgar and Cordelia and supplied a happy ending to satisfy contemporary taste, which recoiled at the death of the innocent heroine in Shakespeare's original play. Not even Garrick, who restored much of the original text in the mid-1750s, dared to reintroduce the Fool, or the death of Cordelia.[15]

Runciman's restoration of the Fool reflected the new interest in Shakespeare's original text on the part of scholars, critics, and editors in the 1760s. In his *Remarks on the Writings and Conduct of J. J. Rousseau* (1767), Henry Fuseli argued that "improvements" of Shakespeare's plays disrupt their tragic unity. In Fuseli's words, Shakespeare "destroys the family of Lear, and wraps Cordelia in the storm" in order to "warn fathers against the dotage of predilection, the fury of prejudice and the destructive consequences of flattery."[16] A Swiss member of the proto-Romantic *Sturm und Drang* movement of nationalist writers and intellectuals, Fuseli had translated *Macbeth* into German before coming to England in 1764. Following his change of profession from writer to artist in the late 1760s, he was to become England's most prolific and influential eighteenth-century artist-interpreter of Shakespeare.

Fuseli was also a great fan of Garrick's. The artist's biographer reported that he attended Garrick's performances regularly, and sat "generally...in the front row of the pit."[17] Two of Fuseli's early drawings, both dating from the mid-1760s, represent Garrick in *Richard III* (Kunsthaus, Zurich) and *Macbeth* (fig. 4). At Reynolds' encouragement, Fuseli spent time in Rome during the 1770s, absorbing the lessons of antiquity and developing a

3. **John Runciman**
King Lear in the Storm, 1767
Oil on panel, 17½ x 24 in., National Gallery of Scotland, Edinburgh

passionate admiration for the art of Michelangelo. He made finished drawings representing scenes from *King Lear, Twelfth Night, Macbeth* and *The Tempest,* and filled many of his sketchbooks with Shakespearean themes, including notes for a scheme to depict some of Shakespeare's characters in a composition based on Michelangelo's Sistine Ceiling (fig. 5). In his writing, Fuseli drew parallels between Michelangelo's protean energy, his expression of spiritual conflict through physical contrapposto, his *terribilità*, and Shakespeare's creative fecundity, his profound insight into human conduct, his dark vision of man's fate.[18]

During his formative years as an artist in Rome, Fuseli continued to develop his views on art, replacing the emphasis on serene, timeless beauty stressed in the theories of Winckelmann, Mengs, Lessing, and Reynolds

4. **Henry Fuseli**
David Garrick and Mrs. Pritchard as Macbeth and Lady Macbeth after the Murder of Duncan
about 1766
Watercolor heightened with white, 12¾ x 15½ in., Funsthaus, Zurich

5. Henry Fuseli
Macbeth
Left: (top) The Murder of Banquo; (bottom) Lady Macbeth Sleepwalking; Center: (top) Macbeth and the Witches; (bottom) Macduff, Lady Macduff, and Her Son; Right: (top) The Murder of Duncan; (bottom) The Three Witches, 1777-78
Ink and brown wash on paper, 10¾ x 7¾ in.
Roman Album, fol. 46v, No. 65, British Museum, London

with an argument for the primacy of expression as a vehicle for stimulating the viewer's imagination.[19] Fuseli's theories expanded upon earlier eighteenth-century philosophers' devaluation of the beautiful in favor of the "sublime," evoked by the threatening aspects of nature, the terror of the immeasurable, the supernatural, the fear of injury or death.[20] Late eighteenth-century critics and artists found an abundance of "sublime" elements in Shakespeare's tragedies: storms, witches, sorcerers, ghosts, dreams, and grisly suicides, murders, and rapes. Among the five Shakespearean themes Fuseli exhibited at the Royal Academy in the 1780s was a scene from *King John* representing Lady Constance refusing to obey the King's summons as she grieves for her thwarted ambitions (cat. no. 24).

During the 1770s and 1780s, interest in Shakespeare burgeoned as philosophers, critics, actors, and artists came into general agreement that he was England's supreme dramatist and poet. Shakespeare's variety ensured his appeal to many different artists, who exhibited a large number of subjects from his plays at the Royal Academy and elsewhere during these decades.[21] The King's History Painter, Benjamin West, essayed several Shakespearean subjects in these years. His lyrical representation of the tender parting scene from *Romeo and Juliet* (cat. no. 63), painted in 1778, stands in marked contrast to Fuseli's dark, brooding image of Lady Constance.

West was among the guests at the dinner party given by Josiah Boydell in 1786 where the idea of a large gallery of paintings devoted to Shakespearean subjects was first conceived. George Romney, another painter fond of Shakespearean themes, was also present. The concept was immediately taken up by Josiah's uncle, Alderman John Boydell, the print publisher who had scored his first big success a decade earlier with the engraving after West's *Death of Wolfe*, the first modern history painting, and who saw in the Shakespeare project a chance to provide encouragement for British history painting through the sale of prints. The pictures were to be housed in a building designed for the purpose, and supported through the sale by subscription of large engravings after them, as well by as a new edition of the plays illustrated with smaller engravings. Boydell was the leading art entrepreneur of his age, and the Shakespeare

6. Henry Fuseli
Titania's Awakening, 1785-89
Oil on canvas, 87⅜ x 110¼ in.
Kunstmuseum, Winterthur

Gallery was his most ambitious undertaking. It first opened to the public in 1789 with 34 pictures; by 1802 there were 167 paintings by 33 different artists. By that time the project, hampered by delays in schedule, financial difficulties, and the halt in continental trade resulting from the Napoleonic Wars, had brought Boydell's firm to the verge of bankruptcy. The Shakespeare Gallery's building and all the pictures were sold by lottery, and later dispersed at auction.[22]

Boydell's stated purpose in commissioning the Gallery was to give British artists an opportunity to compete in the arena of history painting, then considered the noblest category in the hierarchy of art. In selecting an English dramatist as the source for his apotheosis of history painting, Boydell hoped to increase the Shakespeare Gallery's marketability with an appeal to national sentiment. As he wrote in the preface to the catalogue of the first exhibition of the gallery in 1789:

> *In this progress of the fine Arts, though foreigners have allowed our lately acquired superiority of Engraving, and readily admitted the great talents of the principal Painters, yet they have said, with some severity, and, I am sorry to say, with some truth, that the abilities of our best Artists are chiefly employed in painting Portraits of those who, in less than half a century, will be lost in oblivion—While the noblest part of the Art — HISTORICAL PAINTING — is much neglected. To obviate this national reflection was, as I have already hinted, the principal cause of the present undertaking. . . .*[23]

At the outset, Boydell endeavored to obtain pictures from the preeminent painters of the day. He gave the reluctant Reynolds an advance payment of £500 in order to secure his services, but ultimately received only three pictures from him, far fewer than the eight he had sought. Nevertheless, Boydell managed to solicit contributions from almost all the major subject painters of the day, including West, Fuseli, Romney, James Barry, John Hoppner, Angelica Kaufmann, James Northcote, and John Opie. After the initial favorable publicity surrounding these artists' participation had ensured the Shakespeare Gallery's success in attracting subscribers, Boydell turned to less expensive and more readily available artists to complete the project. Among major artists only Fuseli and Northcote contributed as many as nine works, while less well-known men such as Robert Smirke (with 26 contributions), William Hamilton (23), Richard Westall (22) and Francis Wheatley (13) contributed the lion's share of the pictures.

Among the artists of major stature employed in the Shakespeare Gallery scheme, most had studied in Rome, had absorbed the lessons of antiquity and of the Renaissance and Baroque masters, and had aspired to history painting in the grand manner. Of this group, Fuseli, through his art, teaching, and writing, made the greatest impact on the interpretation and iconography of Shake-

7. Joshua Reynolds
The Death of Cardinal Beaufort, about 1789
Engraving by Caroline Watson
Folger Shakespeare Library, Washington, D.C.

speare, whom he called "the supreme master of passions and the ruler of our hearts".[24] Fuseli was fascinated by the irrational and was drawn to scenes incorporating sexuality, dreams, magic, and the supernatural. His grinning, malevolent *Puck* (cat. no. 25), a variation on one of his Boydell Shakespeare Gallery pictures, is accompanied by the tiny sprite Ariel. The same tiny supernatural figure reappears in another of Fuseli's Shakespeare Gallery contributions, *Titania's Awakening* (fig. 6) of 1785-89, which involves dreams, fairies, and metamorphosis. Such images of fantasy and imagination were to exert a strong influence upon nineteenth-century fairy painters. Fuseli's other contributions to the project included representations of Prospero the magician, Macbeth and the Witches, Lear's curse, and a lascivious Falstaff with Doll Tearsheet on his lap.

Many of the weightier contributions to the Boydell Shakespeare Gallery treated "sublime" scenes featuring witches, fairies, madness, or grotesque mutilations or murders.[25] Reynolds painted Macbeth and the Witches, the agonized death of Cardinal Beaufort from *Henry VI, Part II*, (fig. 7) and Puck. West represented Ophelia and Lear (fig. 8) in their mad scenes.[26] Northcote's contributions included a whole series of innocent young victims menaced by brutal armored villains (fig. 9). In *Joan of Arc*

8. **Benjamin West**
King Lear in the Storm, 1788
Oil on canvas, 107 x 144 in.,
Museum of Fine Arts, Boston

and the Furies (cat. no. 28), from *Henry VI, Part I*, William Hamilton adopted the low viewpoint, large-scale muscular figures, unlimited space, and dramatic lighting of Fuseli.

Shakespearean themes were among the earliest painted by another Boydell contributor, George Romney. Two scenes from *King Lear* were among his youthful works sold at a provincial auction in 1762.[27] As a member of Fuseli's circle in Rome he had sketched Shakespearean scenes, and already had several large Shakespearean canvases under way when he attended Josiah Boydell's dinner party in 1786. Romney filled dozens of notebooks with sketches for scenes from the plays, particularly *King Lear, Macbeth,* and *The Tempest,* and the majority of his few completed history paintings represent Shakespearean themes.[28] Like Reynolds, Romney aspired to history painting but earned his living as a portraitist. In his depiction of his close friend John Henderson, then the leading Shakespearean actor, in *Macbeth's Meeting with the Witches* (cat. no. 55), which predates the Boydell Shakespeare Gallery, Romney raised an actor portrait to the level of history painting, emphasizing the horrific, "sublime" elements of the scene. His *The Infant Shakespeare Attended by Nature and the Passions* (cat. no. 56) is an allegorical apotheosis of the Bard himself, and one of the few Boydell Shakespeare pictures that does not illustrate a scene from a play. The varied and exaggerated heads, said to represent Romney's favorite model Emma Hart (later Lady Hamilton) and the performers John Philip Kemble and Sarah Siddons, reflect the shared interest on the part of actors and artists in contemporary theories of expression.[29]

Many of Boydell's major contributors were "grand manner" history painters who looked to sixteenth- and seventeenth-century Italian painting and antique sculpture for their inspiration. A second group, including Robert Smirke and Francis Wheatley, belonged to the native English tradition derived from Hogarth and Francis Hayman, with its roots in Dutch seventeenth-century genre painting. The majority of these artists earned their livings providing designs for book illustrations and popular engravings. As a general but not ironclad rule, history painters preferred Shakespeare's tragedies and darker plays, while genre painters chose scenes from the comedies and lighter episodes from the histories and romances.

The initial success of the Boydell Shakespeare Gallery encouraged other entrepreneurs to assemble, with an eye to engraving, collections of pictures with subjects drawn from various poets, the Bible, and English history.[30] Among these projects was the Irish Shakespeare Gallery, conceived by the printer James Woodmason and exhibited in Dublin in 1793 and later in London.[31] Woodmason employed many of the artists who had contributed to the Boydell Shakespeare Gallery, including Fuseli, Northcote, Opie, Wheatley, William Hamilton, and Matthew William Peters. The illustrated edition of Shakespeare that he planned to publish never appeared, but many of the paintings were later engraved and issued as separate plates.

One of Wheatley's three contributions to the Irish Shakespeare gallery, the melodramatic *Sylvia Rescued by Valentine* (fig. 10), dated 1792, from *The Two Gentlemen of Verona*, depicts Valentine as a lavishly costumed and plumed gallant coming to the aid of his damsel in distress. Wheatley specialized in sentimental domestic genre scenes, many of them painted expressly for the purpose of engraving, and contributed thirteen scenes from Shakespeare's comedies and romances to the Boydell Gallery. Among the Reverend Matthew William Peters'

9. **James Northcote**
Henry VI, Part III, Act I, Scene 3, about 1789
Engraving by C. G. Playter and T. Ryder
Folger Shakespeare Library, Washington, D.C.

10. **Francis Wheatley**
Sylvia Rescued by Valentine, 1792
Oil on canvas, 65½ x 52½ in.,
Yale Center for British Art, New Haven

five contributions to Woodmason's project was *Charmian and the Soothsayer* (cat. no. 48) from *Anthony and Cleopatra*. Peters' Venetian and French influences are evident in his painterly technique, and in the coy rococo grace and plunging décolletage of the principal figure. His reputation as the painter of buxom beauties, who also play dominant roles in three of his four Boydell pictures, was apparently the target of adverse comment from his superiors in the Church.[32] John Opie's *Arthur Taken Prisoner*, (cat. no. 47) from *King John*, another Woodmason picture, exhibits a taste for dark armor and gothic melodrama similar to that found in his and Northcote's Boydell Shakespeare Gallery pictures.

Young artists of the following generation continued to aspire to history painting in the grand manner, but, lacking the generous patronage of a Boydell or a Woodmason, they were forced to appeal to a broader segment of taste. Portrait painters strove to elevate their works by borrowing the expressions, gestures, and compositional devices of history painting while creating salable images of popular Shakespearean actors and actresses, while subject painters deferred to patrons' lack of enthusiasm for the grand manner by working in the more accessible genre mode.

Thomas Lawrence had nursed hopes of becoming a history painter until his large Miltonic subject, *Satan Summoning Up His Legions*, a "sublime" grand manner history painting strongly influenced by Fuseli, proved a failure with the critics at the Royal Academy in 1797. He scored a success in the following year with his portrait of John Philip Kemble as Coriolanus (fig. 11), charging an actor portrait with expressive power by adopting the low viewpoint, monumental figure style, dramatic lighting, and shadowy background associated with Fuseli's history paintings. Lawrence openly acknowledged the compromise in referring to *Kemble as Coriolanus* as "a sort of half-history picture."[33]

Several of Lawrence's pupils also sought in actor portraits an opportunity to achieve some of the impact of history painting while working in a more popular genre. George Henry Harlow's portrait *Mrs. Siddons as Lady Macbeth* (cat. no. 30), exhibited at the British Institution in 1815, reflects the great histrionic power of J. P. Kemble's sister and leading lady, while the actor G. F. Cooke's brilliant impersonation of the conniving, egocentric Richard III informs his portrait by Thomas Sully (cat. no. 60), painted in Philadelphia in 1811 during the British actor's American tour. Sully's father was the leading actor of the American South, and both Sully and Harlow, like their teacher Lawrence, were dedicated theatregoers.

The young American Washington Allston traveled almost 4000 miles from Charleston, South Carolina, to London in 1801 in hopes of becoming a history painter. But when he confided this ambition to Fuseli, the old

11. Thomas Lawrence
John Philip Kemble as Coriolanus, 1798
Oil on canvas, 103 x 70 in., Guildhall Art Gallery, London

man replied, "then you have come *a great way* to starve sir."[34] Even before his trip to London, Allston had known and admired the Boydell Shakespeare prints. During a later stay in Italy he formed a deep and lasting friendship with the great poet and Shakespeare critic Samuel Taylor Coleridge, and, like Fuseli, was profoundly moved by the sublimely expressive art of Michelangelo. But with the notable exception of his unfinished *Death of King John* of 1837, most of Allston's Shakespearean paintings represent romantic and humorous scenes, such as *Falstaff Enlisting his Ragged Regiment* (cat. no. 4) from *Henry IV, Part II*, and *The Opening of the Casket* (cat. no. 5), both modest domestic scenes rendered in a soft, glowing technique derived from the Venetians. Allston's genre pictures are rooted in the native English tradition derived from Hogarth and Hayman. But while genre painters of the previous generation such as Smirke and Wheatley had been forced to take a back seat to grand manner history painters, their nineteenth-century successors enjoyed unprecedented popularity and prestige.

The genre mode was ushered back into favor with the tremendous success at the Royal Academy in 1807 of David Wilkie's *Blind Fiddler*, a humble scene set in rural Scotland and cast in the small scale and domestic style of the seventeenth-century Dutch master Teniers. Further impetus to the trend towards genre pictures came with the exhibitions of Hogarth (1814) and Dutch and Flemish painting (1815). A similar emphasis upon small-scale depictions of domestic scenes from history or literature constructed with scrupulous attention to period details can be seen in the French *style troubadour*, imported into England by Richard Parkes Bonington. His *Anne Page and Slender* (fig. 12) of 1826, from *The Merry Wives of Windsor*, combines an intimate scale and sentimental domestic subject with figures copied directly from an antiquarian costume book.[35] Similar treatments of scenes from literature and history, framed in terms of everyday life and loaded with period details, appeared in the novels of Sir Walter Scott and the histories of Thomas Babington Macaulay, which were well known to the voracious nineteenth-century reading public. By the third decade of the century, artists' interest had shifted almost entirely from the horrific sublime to anecdotal domestic incidents.

This new, more modest approach to subject painting was adopted and developed by Charles Robert Leslie, who had come to London from Philadelphia in 1811 to study with West, and was a member of Allston's circle. His earlier pictures are exercises in the old Romantic "sublime" mode; *The Murder of Rutland by Lord Clifford* (fig. 13), exhibited at the Royal Academy in 1816, treats

12. Richard Parkes Bonington
Anne Page and Slender, 1826
Oil on canvas, 18¾ x 15⅜ in., Wallace Collection, London

Northcote's Boydell Shakespeare Gallery theme (fig. 9) in similar terms of gothic horror. Leslie soon abandoned attempts at grandiose history paintings of weighty subjects and turned to smaller-scale treatments of lighter themes drawn from the writings of Molière, Cervantes, Swift, Goldsmith, and Scott. He exhibited more than a dozen subjects from Shakespeare's comedies and romances, choosing humorous or sentimental themes and placing them in intimate domestic settings, as in the courtship of Anne Page and Slender from *The Merry Wives of Windsor* (fig. 14) exhibited at the Royal Academy in 1825. Following in the footsteps of his teacher West, he undertook extensive research to ensure the accuracy of his period costumes, accessories, furniture, and architecture.

Previously Reynolds, the fervid classicist, had warned against great specificity in the painting of costumes in his seventh *Discourse*, delivered in 1776: "after a time, the dress is only an amusement for an antiquarian; and if it obstructs the general design of the piece, it is to be disregarded by the artist. Common sense must give way to a higher sense. In the naked form, and in the disposition of the drapery, the difference between one artist and another, is principally seen."[36] But these words fell on deaf ears during most of the nineteenth century, as the quest for archaeological authenticity in realizing scenes from the past developed into a consuming obsession. Painstaking research to ensure the correctness of historical costumes and settings came to be considered a vital step in the achievement of literal truth to the past. Artists relied heavily on antiquarian costume books and pursued their own investigations as well, directly consulting illuminated manuscripts, tomb slabs, and old paintings, tapestries, and prints. Period costumes, suits of armor, furniture, and architectural fragments were crammed into their studios and recorded in their sketchbooks. There was much interaction between artists and stage designers, as painters tried their hands at costumes and sets for amateur and professional tableaux and stage productions, or, conversely, clothed their models in dress borrowed or rented from theatrical costumiers.[37]

Artists' interest in Shakespeare reached its peak during the early Victorian period. From the first Royal Academy exhibition in 1769 until 1830, there had been an average of between five and ten Shakespearean subjects each year. In 1830 the number jumped to fifteen, and in the 1840s and 1850s it increased to twenty.[38] The period's great interest in Shakespeare was reflected in the rules for a competition held in 1843, the first of a series organized in connection with the decoration of the new Houses of Parliament. Contributors were required to submit cartoon drawings "executed in chalk or charcoal, not less than ten nor more than fifteen feet in their longest dimension; the figures not to be less than the size of life, illustrating subjects from British History, or from the works of Spenser, Shakespeare, or Milton."[39] Of the

13. **Charles Robert Leslie**
The Murder of Rutland by Lord Clifford, 1815
Oil on canvas, 96¾ x 79½ in.,
Pennsylvania Academy of the Fine Arts, Philadelphia

140 cartoons submitted to the competition, 12 represented Shakespearean themes.[40]

The modest domestic style developed by Wilkie and Leslie found adherents in a group of younger artists known as "The Clique," who came of age around 1830. It was primarily a sketching club which met regularly to draw subjects from Shakespeare and Byron. Of the group's five principal members, Richard Dadd, Augustus Egg, William Powell Frith, Henry Nelson O'Neil, and John Phillip, all but Phillip made notable contributions to the iconography of Shakespeare's plays. Frith made his debut at the Royal Academy in 1840 with *Malvolio before the Countess* (unlocated), from *Twelfth Night,* and continued to paint intimate genre scenes from history and literature. In the 1850s he enlarged his repertoire to include the subjects from modern life, such as *Life at the Seaside: Ramsgate Sands* (1854; Royal Collection, Great Britain) and *Derby Day* (1858, Tate Gallery, London) with which he made his name and fortune. In his autobiography, Frith admitted that he felt more comfortable with subjects from Sterne, Goldsmith, Molière, Cervantes, and *The Spectator* than with Shakespeare, who inspired him with "terror as well as admiration."[41] O'Neil exhibited nearly a dozen themes from Shakespeare's plays, most of them lofty subjects from the tragedies, and an historical reconstruction entitled *Shakespeare Reading a Midsummer Night's Dream to Queen Elizabeth,* shown at the Royal

14. **Charles Robert Leslie**
Slender, with the assistance of Shallow, courting Anne Page, 1825
Oil on canvas, 26¾ x 31½ in.
Yale Center for British Art, New Haven

Academy in 1877. Egg was a talented actor who played in Charles Dickens' amateur productions. His favorite subjects were humorous scenes from Shakespeare, Scott, and Le Sage. He befriended and encouraged the Pre-Raphaelites, and their influence is reflected in his later pictures, such as the scene from *The Taming of the Shrew* (cat. no. 20) of 1860, with its hard, dry handling and strident color contrasts. Richard Dadd is best known today for his fantasy subjects. Elements of the Romantic sublime persist in Dadd's early, jewel-like *Titania Sleeping* (cat. no. 14), from *A Midsummer Night's Dream*. Exhibited at the Royal Academy in 1841, this picture was strongly influenced by the earlier example of Fuseli (see fig. 6). Insanity ran in Dadd's family, and in 1843 the artist murdered his father in a fit of madness. He was confined to asylums for the rest of his life, but his physicians encouraged him to continue with his art, and he developed a distinctive taut, linear style characterized by strange staring figures and flat, telescoped compositions. His great Shakespearean masterpiece, the enigmatic *Contradiction: Oberon and Titania* (fig. 15) from *A Midsummer Night's Dream*, was painted at Bethlem Hospital in the mid-1850s.

Fairy painting constituted a major branch of Victorian art, and Shakespeare's two fairy plays, *A Midsummer Night's Dream* and *The Tempest*, proved fertile ground for artists in search of fairy subjects. Ultimately derived from Fuseli (fig. 6) and the late eighteenth-century fascination with the supernatural as one aspect of the "sublime," fairy painting was stimulated by the Romantics' interest in exploring the indigenous national past, by the desire for escape from the utilitarian modern world, and by the Victorian fashion for spiritualism.[42]

The fairy cult was manifested on the stage in elaborate pageants and spectacles, as in Charles Kean's enormously popular production of *A Midsummer Night's Dream*, which opened in 1856 and enjoyed a long run. Fairy stories, of course, abound in Victorian literature, from the first translation into English of the Grimms' fairy tales, issued in 1823-24 with illustrations by George Cruikshank, to the publication of J. M. Barrie's *Peter Pan* in 1904.

The fairy tradition enjoyed an equally long life in painting, from Fuseli through Daniel Maclise's *The Disenchantment of Bottom* (cat. no. 42) of 1832, from *A Midsummer Night's Dream*, to Arthur Rackham's *Wedding Scene* from the same play (fig. 16), dated 1908. Joseph Noel Paton, one of the best-known Victorian fairy painters, published a book of outline drawings from Shakespeare's *Tempest* in 1845, and drew the illustrations for an edition of Shakespeare's plays published in 1868. In 1847 Paton exhibited a large *Reconciliation of Oberon and Titania* (National Gallery of Scotland, Edinburgh) at the Royal Scottish Academy; its companion *Quarrel of Oberon and Titania* (fig. 17), followed in 1850. If Paton's interest in magic and the supernatural looks back to Fuseli, his careful transcription of natural details prefigures one of the dominant trends of the 1850s. Paton befriended the young Pre-Raphaelite John Everett Millais, whose *Ferdinand Lured by Ariel* (fig. 18) from *The Tempest*, exhibited at the Royal Academy in 1850, raised fairy painting to a new level of verisimilitude.

Illustrated editions of Shakespeare's plays, first produced during the eighteenth century, reached the peak of their popularity during the mid-Victorian period. From the roughly twenty illustrated editions published in the first decade of the century, the number rose to a high of fifty

15. **Richard Dadd**
Contradiction: Oberon and Titania, 1854-58
Oil on canvas, oval, 24 x 29½ in.
Private collection

during the 1850s, then gradually fell back to twenty by the 1890s.[43] Boydell's ideal of publication as a means of encouraging a national school of history painting fell by the wayside as publishers sought to capture a wider market. Sweet, attractive young females thinly disguised as Shakespeare's heroines appear in the publications of Charles Heath, the engraver and principal promoter of the illustrated annual collections of verse and prose known as "keepsake" books. Heath's *Shakespeare Gallery, containing the principal Female characters in the plays of the great poet* (1836-37), and *Heroines of Shakespeare* (1848), are collections of steel engravings after "keepsake" portraits by Leslie, Frith, Egg, and others. Idealized single female figures from Shakespeare achieved enormous popularity. They were a sub-specialty of Thomas Frank Dicksee (cat. no. 19), who exhibited more than a dozen female characters from Shakespeare at the Royal Academy during the second half of the century, and who contributed illustrations to Mary Cowden Clarke's sentimental and moralizing *The Girlhood of Shakespeare's Heroines in a Series of Tales* (1881). Fashionable portrait painters like James Sant (cat. no. 58) made occasional forays into Shakespearean territory with similar heroines.[44]

The Victorian penchant for trivializing and sentimentalizing Shakespeare's solemn subjects is epitomized in Charles Hunt's *My 'Macbeth'* (cat. no. 34), dated 1863. A portrait of the artist with his wife and son, the picture celebrates the joys of domestic comfort and family life. Hunt shows himself pointing to the picture he exhibited at the Royal Academy in 1864, in which one of Shakespeare's grimmest plays is reduced to a humorous genre scene of young children acting out the

16. **Arthur Rackham**
The Wedding Scene in A Midsummer Night's Dream, 1908
Watercolor and ink on paper, 10½ x 7¼ in., Folger Shakespeare Library, Washington, D.C.

17. Joseph Noel Paton
The Quarrel of Oberon and Titania, 1849
Oil on canvas, 39 x 60 in.,
National Gallery of Scotland, Edinburgh

banquet scene in makeshift costumes (including a bedsheet for the ghost of Banquo) before an audience of their peers.

The development early in the nineteenth century of relief wood engraving, which was faster and therefore cheaper to produce than intaglio steel engraving, as well as capable of being locked together with the type elements for inking and printing, revolutionized the publishing industry and changed the look of the printed page. Of the many mid-Victorian editions of Shakespeare's plays, the outstanding monument was the edition of 1856-58 with more than 800 designs by John Gilbert, engraved in wood by the Dalziel Brothers. Gilbert was a phenomenally prolific illustrator associated with the *Illustrated London News*, and he produced literally thousands of drawings for illustrated editions of works by Cowper, Scott, Wordsworth, Milton, and Cervantes. His facility as a draughtsman was legendary, and in marked contrast to his contemporaries, he required neither models, costumes, nor archaeological research to complete his pictures, but worked from his prodigious memory, spurred on by a bit of engraved silver for armor or scraps of velvet and brocade for costumes. Gilbert also worked in oil and watercolor, and exhibited more than 50 Shakespearean subjects at the Old Water Color Society. His *The Plays of William Shakespeare* (cat. no. 26) of 1849, teeming with dozens of characters, is a Rubensian celebration of bardolatry gone wild, a pictorial equivalent of Garrick's Shakespeare festival of nearly a century earlier.

The Victorian tendency to canonize Shakespeare's characters extended even to the contriving of their "biographies," as in Clarke's tales of the heroines as children. George Cruikshank's *Pistol Informing Falstaff of the Death of Henry IV* (cat. no. 12) was drawn for Richard B. Brough's *Life of Sir John Falstaff*, published in 1857-58. Depictions of Shakespeare himself were also popular. John Faed's *Shakespeare and His Contemporaries* (cat. no. 23) shows the Bard surrounded by fellow luminaries, including Francis Bacon, Ben Jonson, and John Donne. Posed as if for a photograph, the picture reflects the nineteenth century's interest in historical portraits, which led to the founding of the National Portrait Gallery in London in 1856.[45]

The anecdotal and historicizing approach to Shakespeare practiced by Leslie and the members of the Clique characterizes most mid-century depictions of scenes from

18. John Everett Millais
Ferdinand Lured by Ariel, 1849-50
Oil on panel, 25½ x 20 in., Makins Collection

19. **John Everett Millais**
Ophelia, 1851-52
Oil on canvas, top corners rounded, 30 x 44 in., Tate Gallery, London

the plays. Alfred Elmore's representation of a scene from *Much Ado About Nothing* (cat. no. 21), signed and dated 1846, is probably *The Fainting of Hero* that Elmore exhibited at the Royal Academy in that year. It shows the mock-tragic moment from the play when Hero, unfairly rejected at the altar by her betrothed, falls into a death-like swoon. Elmore orchestrated nearly a score of figures into a complex composition, but his interest in the varied reactions of the protagonists and spectators, and the painstaking exactitude with which he painted the rich period costumes and accessories, point to his ultimate dependence upon the domestic genre mode. A weightier subject receives similar treatment in terms of anecdote and archaeology in E. M. Ward's *King Lear and Cordelia* (cat. no. 62) where, despite the spectacular elaboration of the scene with lavish fabrics and accessories, the accompaniment of musicians, and a breathtaking glimpse of the white cliffs of Dover, the central focus remains upon the tender relationship of father and daughter. Daniel Maclise's *The Play Scene from 'Hamlet'* (cat. no. 40), the original version of which was exhibited at the Royal Academy in 1842, belongs to the same narrative and historicizing vein although it attains a certain epic grandeur through its monumental scale, tight compositional scheme, dramatic chiaroscuro, and complex allegorical symbolism.

Shakespeare's plays provided a vital source of inspiration for the young Pre-Raphaelites, who first came together in 1848.[46] Of the initial seven members of the group, the most important were William Holman Hunt, John Everett Millais, and Dante Gabriel Rossetti. Shakespeare ranked high in their list of "Immortals," and they called for the celebration of his birthday as a national holiday.[47] Inspired by the critic John Ruskin's call for young artists to "go to Nature in all singleness of heart,...rejecting nothing, selecting nothing, and scorning nothing...," the Pre-Raphaelites developed an obsession with minute accuracy in natural details.[48] In painting their landscape backgrounds outdoors, in bright natural light, they achieved a striking new realism imbued with freshness and clarity, as well as a novel, profound symbolism born of the juxtaposition of their figures with elements from the natural world.[49] For the Pre-Raphaelites, painstaking research into the period details of costumes and accessories was concomitant to botanical exactitude.[50] Rejecting the open brushwork and anecdotal approach of their predecessors, they chose darker moments from Shakespeare's plays that allowed them to explore more complex thematic and psychological issues, and turned to fifteenth-century Flemish and Italian art as sources for their deliberately awkward figure style. In insisting that "the naive traits of frank expression and unaffected grace were what had made Italian art so essentially vigorous and progressive, until the showy followers of Michael Angelo had grafted their Dead Sea fruit on to the vital tree," they categorically rejected the prevailing theories of beauty and expression, derived from High Renaissance and Baroque precedents, that had governed British art since their codification by Reynolds and Fuseli nearly a century earlier.[51]

Millais spent six months and more than a thousand hours outdoors painting the background of his *Ophelia* (fig. 19) from *Hamlet*, exhibited at the Royal Academy in 1852. His model posed for many days in a bathtub to ensure the accuracy of his depiction of the floating body. In selecting a scene that is described but not staged in the play, he avoided hackneyed theatrical stereotypes. As in many early Pre-Raphaelite paintings, space is compressed to an almost two-dimensional flatness, and there is an obsessive attention to botanical detail. Millais' model was Elizabeth Siddal, a cockney girl discovered by his friend Walter Deverell in a hat shop. Before taking up with Rossetti and becoming his exclusive model, and later his wife, she essayed several other Shakespearean

20. **William Holman Hunt**
Valentine Rescuing Sylvia From Proteus
1850-51
Oil on canvas, arched top, 38¾ x 52½ in.
Birmingham Museum and Art Gallery
Birmingham, England

roles for the Pre-Raphaelites and their circle in the early 1850s, appearing as Sylvia in Holman Hunt's *Valentine Rescuing Sylvia from Proteus* (fig. 20) from *The Two Gentlemen of Verona*, exhibited at the Royal Academy in 1851, and as Viola in Deverell's *Twelfth Night* (cat. no. 17), shown at the National Institution in 1850. Hunt selected one of the few sinister scenes from a comedy noted for its light, entertaining mood, and placed his figures, locked in a struggle with heavily sexual, moralizing overtones, into a minutely observed natural world. Deverell's picture, with its smaller scale, festive mood, delicately drawn, diminutive figures, and architectonic, stagelike space, directly reflects the Pre-Raphaelites' interest in Quattrocento painting.

The Pre-Raphaelites' penchant for self-absorbed women and for the meticulous transcription of leaves, flowers, and stone walls exerted a powerful influence upon many English artists of the 1850s. Younger artists were especially vulnerable, but even some of the older generation responded to its attractions. For example, the profusion of minutely stippled leaves and flowers surrounding the principal figures in Henry Anelay's watercolor of Ferdinand and Miranda (cat. no. 6) from *The Tempest*, exhibited at the Royal Watercolor Society in 1852, parallels the Pre-Raphaelites' passion for minute botanical details. Another case in point is that of F. R. Pickersgill, born nearly a decade earlier than the members of the Brotherhood. In his *Viola and the Countess* (cat. no. 50) from *Twelfth Night*, dated 1859, the flesh painting retains an academic solidity, but the two soulful women inhabit a private world, and the landscape elements are described with great specificity.

The "costume picture," in which a painter displayed his erudition in matters of historical dress, accessories, and architecture in a technique of detailed realism, retained its popularity until the end of the century. A dress plays the starring role in Wolfgang Boehm's *A Scene from 'The Taming of the Shrew'* (cat. no. 7), as Petruchio displays the beautiful gown that he has had made to tantalize Katherine, but that he will reject and return to the tailor. The exaggerated emphasis on the reactions of the various characters and their frieze-like arrangement in the shallow, stage-like space place the picture firmly in the genre tradition. For *Othello Recounting His Adventures to Desdemona* (cat. no. 32) of 1869, Robert Alexander Hillingford chose a sentimental courtship scene from a tragic play. The influence of Venetian art, especially Veronese, is evident in the stage-like space with its rear balcony, in the contrast of the dark Moor with his pale wife, and in the rich juxtapositions of luxurious fabrics, laces, and armor, all painted in a mellow glazing technique.

The mid-nineteenth-century interest in elaborate anecdotal compositions rendered with meticulous attention to period detail was an international one, occupying the late Nazarenes and their followers in Germany and the descendants of David and Ingres, notably Delaroche, Gérôme and Meissonier in France. The German-American Emmanuel Leutze received a Nazarene-style education at the Academy in Dusseldorf, and remained in that city for most of his life, but he painted dozens of subjects from British history and literature resembling those of his British contemporaries, and drawn from the same sources, such as Scott and Macaulay. Leutze's scene from *The Merry Wives of Windsor* (cat. no. 38), a late work painted in 1865, after his return to the United States, displays his Anglophilia and shows his ability to research and manipulate details of architecture and costume in a manner similar to those of his French and British counterparts.

21. **William Holman Hunt**
Claudio and Isabella, 1850-53, retouched 1879
Oil on panel, 30½ x 18 in., Tate Gallery, London

Wladyslaw Czachorski, a Polish artist active in Munich, employed decor and costumes skillfully in his carefully constructed and elaborately detailed *Players Before Hamlet* (cat. no. 13), which won a gold medal at the International Exhibition in Munich in 1879. Czachorski combines psychology with pageantry in building the scene around the contrast between the brooding Hamlet with his courtiers, all clad in somber tones, and the extroverted players in their flamboyant costumes.

During the 1860s, 1870s, and 1880s, the number of Shakespearean subjects exhibited at the Royal Academy declined slightly, from an average of twenty to about fifteen a year,[52] but Shakespeare continued to serve artists working in the diverse stylistic traditions that characterized British painting of the late nineteenth century. The anecdotal genre tradition descended from C. R. Leslie survived in the work of the St. John's Wood Clique, a group of artists who came together in the 1860s, living in close proximity to each other in the St. John's Wood section of London, and gathering at each other's houses every Saturday to draw from literary and historical subjects.[53] The Clique's official membership included Philip Hermogenes Calderon, John Evan Hodgson, George Dunlop Leslie (the son of C. R. Leslie), Henry Stacy Marks, George Adolphus Storey, William Frederick Yeames, and David Wilkie Wynfield. They achieved immense popularity with anecdotal scenes from Shakespeare, the middle ages, and British history, and became a powerful force at the Royal Academy. The group was jovial and high-spirited, fond of presenting amateur musicals and dramas, comic sermons, and tableaux. One of their favorite meeting places was Hodgson's studio, which they decorated with a series of mostly Shakespearean frescoes.

Many of the members of the St. John's Wood Clique fell under the spell of Pre-Raphaelitism early in their careers. *Dogberry Examining Conrade and Borachio* (cat. no. 44) and *Bardolph* (cat. no. 43), two of Stacy Marks' earliest contributions to Royal Academy exhibitions, combine Pre-Raphaelite precision of line and clarity of detail with his predilection for comic characters, far removed from the somber, portentuous mood of most Pre-Raphaelite treatments of Shakespeare's plays. A notorious practical joker, Marks was partial to humorous characters like Christopher Sly, Slender, Francis Feeble, and Bottom. He exhibited more than a dozen Shakespearean subjects at the Royal Academy.

Calderon's *The Young Lord Hamlet* (cat. no. 9) of 1868 is a striking example of the Victorian ability to extract a comic scene even from an unrelievedly grim soliloquy, and, as in Hunt's *My 'Macbeth'* (cat. no. 34) of 1863, the transformation from tragedy to comedy is achieved through a sentimental focus upon childhood. Unlike Marks, Calderon also had his serious side. In *A Scene from 'Measure for Measure'* (cat. no. 8), another incident mentioned but not staged in the play, Mariana pleads with her hard-hearted fiancé Angelo, who has rejected her upon learning that her dowry was lost at sea with her brother's ship. The picture bears comparison with Holman Hunt's *Claudio and Isabella* from the same play, exhibited at the Royal Academy in 1853 (fig. 21), in which Isabella refuses to save her brother's life by sacrificing her virginity to the hypocritical Angelo, who has condemned him to death for fornication. Calderon's picture features a lush outdoor setting, richer costumes, and more melodramatic gestures and expressions than Hunt's stark interior prison scene, but both artists depict private tragedies in intimate terms, avoiding the anecdotal domestic approach in favor of a more psychologically penetrating art.

One major late Victorian artist-interpreter of Shakespearean themes was Edwin Austin Abbey. Born in Philadelphia in 1852, he spent his early career in New York as an illustrator for Harper and Brothers. In 1878 he was sent to Stratford-upon-Avon to illustrate an article

22. **Edwin Austin Abbey**
Richard, Duke of Gloucester, and the Lady Anne
1896
Oil on canvas, 52½ x 104¼
Yale University Art Gallery, New Haven

on Shakespeare's birthplace, and stayed on as Harper's English correspondent. In 1887, at the suggestion of his editor, he began a series of pen-and-ink drawings to illustrate Shakespeare's comedies. These were published in *Harper's Monthly* accompanied by critical essays by Andrew Lang, and reprinted in a four-volume edition of the plays published by Harper's in 1899. A series of illustrations to the tragedies (cat. no. 3) and histories, with essays by various authors, followed in *Harper's Monthly*, but the planned companion edition of these plays was never issued.

Not until relatively late in life, about the time of his marriage in 1890 at the age of 38 to a wealthy and ambitious New York heiress, did Abbey begin to paint seriously in oil. His first major Shakespearean work in that medium, *Richard, Duke of Gloucester, and the Lady Anne* (fig. 22) from *Richard III*, was acclaimed as picture of the year at the Royal Academy in 1896 and led to his election to Associate membership in the Academy. During the next ten years, Abbey went on to exhibit half-a-dozen more monumental Shakespearean canvases, including the emotionally charged, crowded and stylized *Penance of Eleanor, Duchess of Gloucester* (cat. no. 2) of 1900.

Abbey's youthful admiration for the art of the Pre-Raphaelites, Rossetti in particular, can be seen in his choice of portentous or lyrical scenes from the plays, and in his emphasis upon historical authenticity, buttressed by a vast amount of research in museums and galleries, an impressive library of reference books, and a huge personal costume collection. Abbey preferred Shakespearean scenes set in the middle ages or the Renaissance that allowed him to explore themes of innocence and betrayal, chivalry and romance, and enabled him to paint the suits of armor and the loose, voluminous garments beloved of the Aesthetic movement. Until the end of his life, Abbey's work retained the strong narrative elements and intimate connection with the text characteristic of the illustrator's art.

Close parallels to Abbey's complex, multifigured compositions, his combining of historical exactitude with pictorial brilliance, his love of pageantry, and his emphasis upon heightened psychological states (cat. no. 1) can be seen in the Shakespearean productions of Henry Irving, the king of the late Victorian stage. Irving acknowledged the kinship between Abbey's art and his own when he recreated *Richard, Duke of Gloucester, and the Lady Anne* (fig. 22) as a living picture in his 1896 production of the play,[54] and later, in 1898, when he commissioned Abbey to design the costumes for an aborted production of *Richard II*.[55]

Edwin Long's portrait of Irving as Richard III (cat. no. 39), painted in 1877, early in the actor's career, captures the sharp ironic villainy with which Irving played the role, and records his splendid costume of satin, velvet, fur, and jewels. Endowed with neither a handsome face, an imposing physique, nor a powerful voice, Irving fashioned his tremendous appeal as an actor from his ability to enter into the mental states of Shakespeare's characters with great intensity, and increased his popularity with lavish productions that sparkled with archaeological authenticity and pictorial splendor.

As the nineteenth century drew to a close, critical enthusiasm for Irving's wholehearted pursuit of scenic illusion declined; Shakespeare scholars and critics came increasingly to feel that such pomp and splendor distracted from the appreciation of Shakespeare's subtler points and deeper meanings. The literal historicism that had been an article of faith among actors and figure painters throughout much of the nineteenth century came increasingly under attack as the new generation's interest shifted to the manipulation of form and color for its own sake and to the exploration of inner realities.[56]

One significant development in late nineteenth-century artists' approaches to Shakespeare is epitomized in the evolution of the art of Frederic Leighton. As a young painter fresh from a Nazarene training in Berlin, he produced *The Reconciliation of the Montagues and the Capulets* in 1854 (fig. 23). This watercolor reflects the composition of a major oil painting (Agnes Scott College, Decatur, Georgia) that was begun in 1853 and exhibited at the Exposition Universelle in Paris in 1855. Its painstaking historical reconstructions and complex multifigured composition is typical of mid-century history

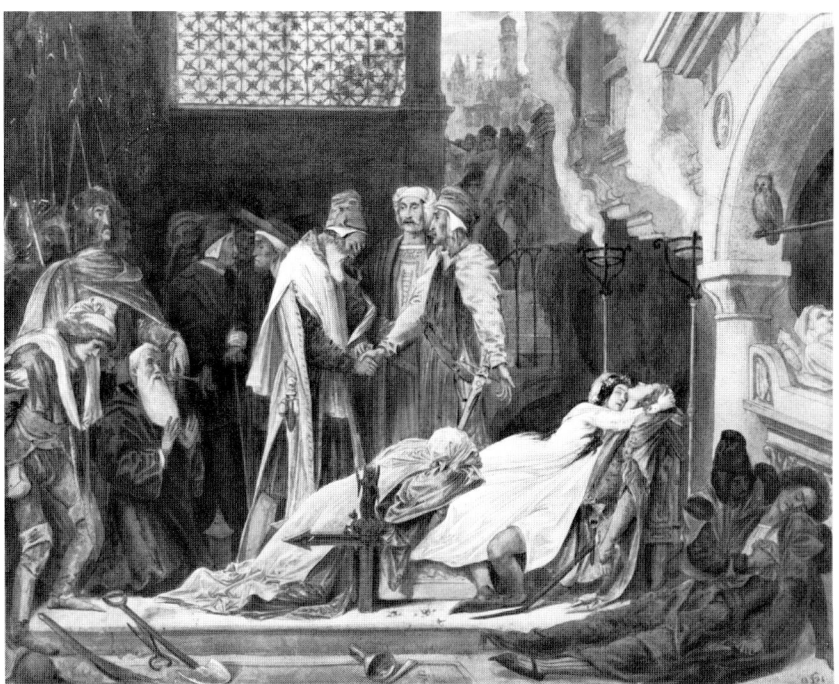

23. Frederic Leighton
The Reconciliation of the Montagues and the Capulets, 1854
Pencil, watercolor, and bodycolor on paper, 15½ x 20½ in., Yale Center for British Art, New Haven

painting. Leighton gradually came to reject the meticulous research into costumes and settings and the elaborate theatrical narratives that had characterized English representations from Shakespeare and other subjects from the time of the Boydell Shakespeare Gallery. As he wrote his teacher Edward von Steinle in 1864:

> I must candidly confess that I cannot agree about a complete illustration of the Shakespearian [sic] plays, those masterpieces already in existence as exhaustively finished works of art; it seems to me that in literature only those subjects lend themselves to pictorial representation which stand in written work more as suggestion. Subjects perhaps which are provided in the Bible or in mythology and tradition in great variety, or are not already generally in the possession of the minds of the spectators of living plays. (e.g. the Greek Tragedies.) It is for the most part a struggle with the incomparable, already existing complete—which is quite intimidating to my capabilities.[57]

Leighton's later Shakespearean subjects are limited to portrayals of lovely young women as studies in form, color, and mood, with titles such as *Viola* (fig. 24) and *Bianca* (Royal Collection, Great Britain). In 1888 he contributed a *Desdemona* (private collection, Great Britain) to the *Graphic Heroines of Shakespeare* series, the late Victorian successor to Charles Heath's "keepsake" albums.[58]

In E.R. Hughes' meticulously detailed watercolor, *The Shrew Katherina* (cat. no. 33) of 1896, the earlier emphasis upon the details of costume, props, and accessories still remains, but the narrative element so pronounced in Boehm's representation from the same play (cat. no. 7) is drained away and the single female figure becomes an almost purely decorative element with little or no inherent drama. Her pensive, inward-looking quality cannot be related to a particular scene in the play; ultimately derived from Rossetti's introspective women, it is characteristic of much art of the Aesthetic movement.[59]

During the 1880s and 1890s, many young British artists were strongly attracted to French painting, especially the art of Jules Bastien-Lepage. Even before his *Joan of Arc Listening to the Voices* (Metropolitan Museum of Art, New York) was exhibited to great controversy and acclaim at the Salon of 1880, Bastien-Lepage's work had been shown in London, and he had attracted British followers. Two separate groups, known as the Newlyn School and the Glasgow School, emulated his monumental peasant subjects, his combining of painterly outdoor naturalism with solid academic figure drawing, and his cool greenish-gray tonalities.[60] In *Ophelia and Laertes* (cat. no. 27), dated 1885, the young Maurice Greiffenhagen adapted Bastien-Lepage's painterly technique, chalky tones, and exploration of intense psychological states to a Shakespearean theme, combining it with the taste for medieval subjects and for flattened, decorative spatial treatment characteristic of Rossetti's Aesthetic followers. The embroidered curtain in the background of Greiffenhagen's picture, based on the Bayeux Tapestry, reflects the revival of interest in medieval needlework by the Arts and Crafts movement.[61] *Ophelia and Laertes* is probably the "subject from *Hamlet*" that Greiffenhagen submitted to a competition for a gold medal and travelling scholarship sponsored by the Royal Academy schools in the mid-1880s. According to a friend, he placed only second despite widespread admiration for his painting because the judges were determined not to encourage the growing "Frenchy" tendency among the students.[62] From the late 1880s

24. **Frederic Leighton**
Viola, about 1881
Oil on canvas, 18⅞ x 13¼ in.,
Private collection, New York

Greiffenhagen exhibited with the New English Art Club, an uneasy alliance of the British and Scottish followers of Bastien-Lepage with the "London Impressionists," led by Walter Sickert.

Literary content, subverted by Leighton and by many of the artists of the Aesthetic movement, was jettisoned altogether by Sickert and his friends, who revered the art of Whistler and painted modern life subjects in the spirit of Degas and Monet. In the work of the "London Impressionists," the crude vitality of the music hall superseded the lavish historical reconstructions of the era of Irving and Abbey. The Sickert contingent gained the upper hand at the New English Art Club during the 1890s, as the followers of Bastien-Lepage gradually defected to the Royal Academy. By the outbreak of the first World War, French modernism had prevailed in England. Narrative and anecdotal costume pictures lost their compelling meaning for all but a few elderly Victorians, and the grand tradition of Shakespearean painting that had flourished for nearly a century and a half died out.

Between the two World Wars, art-historical interest in late eighteenth- and nineteenth-century British academic painting was barely kept alive by a small group of scholars and critics. The publication after the second World War of John Ironside and Robin Gere's *Pre-Raphaelite Painters* (1948), and of Graham Reynolds' *Painters of the Victorian Scene* (1953), set into motion a new reevaluation of nineteenth-century English art. By the 1960s, Victorian painting was attracting another generation of British and American academics, museum curators, and connoisseurs. Today, many artists are turning to figurative modes, hundreds of scholars are devoting their lives to the study of academic art, and museums and private collectors are eagerly acquiring and exhibiting examples of such work. With the revival of interest in literary painting, the study of Shakespearean art is finally enjoying a belated but well-deserved resurrection.[63]

NOTES

1. For a detailed discussion of the history of this controversy, see Carol J. Carlisle, "The Nineteenth-Century Actors *versus* the Closet Critics of Shakespeare," *Studies in Philology*, 51 (1954), pp. 599-615.

2. Charles Lamb, "On the Tragedies of Shakespeare, Considered with Reference to their Fitness for Stage Representation," (1811), in *The Works of Charles and Mary Lamb*, ed. E. V. Lucas, 1903-05, I, p. 98.

3. Charles Lamb to Samuel Rogers, probably December 21, 1833, in *The Letters of Charles Lamb*, ed. E. V. Lucas, New Haven, 1935, III, p. 394.

4. Henry Irving, "Shakespeare as a Playwright," in *The Works of William Shakespeare*, ed. Henry Irving and Frank A. Marshall, New York, 1890, I, pp. lxxvii, lxxxi.

5. William Moelwyn Merchant and Ronald Pickvance, *Shakespeare in Art: Paintings, Drawings and Engravings Devoted to Shakespearean Subjects*, exh. cat., Arts Council of Great Britain, 1964, p. 6.

6. Geoffrey Ashton, *Shakespeare's Heroines in the Nineteenth Century*, exh. cat., Buxton Museum and Art Gallery, Buxton, England, 1980, p. iv.

7. Esther Gordon Dotson, "Shakespeare Illustrated, 1770-1820," PhD Dissertation, Institute of Fine Arts, New York University, 1972, p. ii.

8. The plays were edited by Samuel Johnson, 1765; George Steevens, 1766; and Edward Capell, 1767-68; and interpreted in Henry Home, Lord Kames, *Elements of Criticism*, Edinburgh, 1762; Richard Hurd, *Letters on Chivalry and Romance*, London, 1762, and Elizabeth Montagu, *Essay on the Writings and Genius of Shakespear* [sic], London, 1769; see Dotson, 1972, pp. 1-2, note 1.

9. Dotson, 1972, pp. 1-6.

10. Christian Deelman, *The Great Shakespeare Jubilee*, London, 1964; Martha Winburn England, *Garrick's Jubilee*, [Columbus, Ohio], 1964; Johanne M. Stochholm, *Garrick's Folly*, New York, 1964.

11. Lance Bertelsen, "David Garrick and English Painting," *Eighteenth-Century Studies* 11 (1978), pp. 308-24.

12. Joshua Reynolds, *Discourses on Art*, ed. Robert R. Wark, San Marino, 1959.

13. David Goodreau, *Nathaniel Dance, 1735-1811*, exh. cat., Iveagh Bequest, Kenwood, 1977, n.p., no. 16. After deserting his wife and family, and his law career, for the life of an itinerant actor, James Dance assumed an anglicized version of the name of his companion, Catherine L'Amour. See Dorothy Stroud, *George Dance, Architect*, London, 1971, p. 47.

14. William Moelwyn Merchant, "John Runciman's 'Lear in the Storm'," *Journal of the Warburg and Courtauld Institutes* 17 (1954), pp. 385-87, revised in idem, *Shakespeare and the Artist*, London, 1959, pp. 190-98.

15. See Montague Summers, *Shakespeare Adaptations*, London, 1922.

16. Excerpted in Eudo C. Mason, *The Mind of Henry Fuseli*, London, 1951, p. 170.

17. John Knowles, *The Life and Writings of Henry Fuseli*, London, 1831, I. p. 39.

18. See Dotson, 1972, p. 435-37.

19. Johann Joachim Winckelmann, *Gedanken über die Nachamung der greicheschen Werke in der Malerei und Bildhauerkunst*, Dresden, 1755, translated by Fuseli as *Reflections on the Painting and Sculpture of the Greeks*, London, 1765; Anton Raphael Mengs, *Gedanken über die Schönheit und den Geschmack in der Mahlerey*, Zurich, 1762; Gotthold Ephraim Lessing, *Laokoön*, Berlin, 1766; Reynolds, ed. Wark, 1959; cited and discussed in Dotson, 1972, p. 435, note 372.

20. See especially Edmund Burke, *A Philosophical Enquiry into the Origin of Our Ideas of the Sublime and Beautiful*, 1757, in *The Works of the Right Honourable Edmund Burke*, Dublin, I, 1792, pp. 63-250.

21. See Dotson, 1972, pp. 494-504, Appendix B: "Subjects from Shakespeare in the exhibits of the artists' societies from their inception through 1830."

22. On the Boydell Shakespeare Gallery, see Winifred Friedman, *Boydell's Shakespeare Gallery*, PhD Dissertation, Harvard University, 1974, published New York, 1976; Richard W. Hutton and Laura Nelke, *Alderman Boydell's Shakespeare Gallery: An Exhibition of a Selection of the Engravings Made after the Paintings...*, exh. cat., David and Alfred Smart Gallery, University of Chicago, 1978.

23. Quoted in *The Boydell Shakespeare Prints*, intro. by A. E. Santaniello, New York, 1968, n.p.

24. Lecture III, in Knowles, 1831, II, p. 145.

25. All of the Boydell Shakespeare Gallery engravings are conveniently reproduced in Santaniello, 1968.

26. See Judy Sund, "Benjamin West: A Scene from *King Lear*," *Bulletin of the Detroit Institute of Arts* 58 (1980), pp. 127-36.

27. John Romney, *Memoirs of the Life and Works of George Romney*, London, 1830, pp. 24-26.

28. Many of Romney's sketchbooks containing Shakespearean subjects are in the Fitzwilliam Museum, Cambridge University, and at the Folger Shakespeare Library, Washington, D.C. See Patricia Jaffe, *Drawings by George Romney*, exh. cat., Fitzwilliam Museum, Cambridge University, 1977.

29. See Alastair Smart, "Dramatic Gesture and Expression in the Age of Hogarth and Reynolds," *Apollo* 82 (1965), pp. 90-97.

30. On Thomas Macklin's Poets' Gallery and illustrated Bible, and Robert Bowyer's illustrated edition of Hume's *History of England*, see T. S. R. Boase, "Macklin and Bowyer," *Journal of the Warburg and Courtauld Institutes* 26 (1963), pp. 148-77.

31. See Robin Hamlyn, "An Irish Shakespeare Gallery," *Burlington Magazine* 120 (1978), pp. 515-29.

32. Lady Victoria Manners, *Matthew William Peters, R. A.: His Life and Work*, London, 1913, p. 24.

33. Quoted in D. E. Williams, *The Life and Correspondence of Sir Thomas Lawrence*, London, 1831, I, p. 197.

34. Quoted in William Dunlap, *History of the Rise and Progress of the Arts of Design in the United States*, New York, 1834; rpt. New York, 1965, II, p. 306.

35. Roy Strong, *Recreating the Past: British History and the Victorian Painter*, New York, 1978, p. 89.

36. Reynolds, ed. Wark, 1959, p. 128.

37. See Strong, 1978; Sara Stevenson and Helen Bennett, *Van Dyck in Check Trousers: Fancy Dress in Art and Life, 1700-1900*, exh. cat., Scottish National Portrait Gallery, Edinburgh, 1978.

38. Ashton, 1980, p. iv.

39. T. S. R. Boase, "The Decoration of the New Palace of Westminster," *Journal of the Warburg and Courtauld Institutes* 17 (1954), p. 324.

40. Ibid., p. 327.

41. William P. Frith, *My Autobiography and Reminiscences*, London, 1887, I, p. 152.

42. See Jeremy Maas, *Victorian Painters*, New York, 1969, ch. 10: "Fairy Painters"; Diana L. Johnson, *Fantastic Illustration and Design in Britain, 1850-1930*, exh. cat., Rhode Island School of Design, Providence, 1979.

43. Ashton, 1980, p. iv.

44. On the Victorian obsession with Shakespeare's heroines, see Ashton, 1980.

45. See Strong, 1978, p. 62.

46. For a list of representations of scenes from Shakespeare's plays by the Pre-Raphaelites, see Christine Poulson, "A Checklist of Pre-Raphaelite Illustrations of Shakespeare's Plays," *Burlington Magazine* 122 (1980), pp. 244-50.

47. Dante Gabriel Rossetti to William Michael Rossetti, August 30, 1848, quoted in William Michael Rossetti, *Dante Gabriel Rossetti: His Family-Letters, with a Memoir*, London, 1895, II, p. 42; W. Holman Hunt, *Pre-Raphaelitism and the Pre-Raphaelite Brotherhood*, London, 1905, I, pp. 110-12.

48. John Ruskin, *Modern Painters*, I, 1843, in *The Works of John Ruskin*, ed. E. T. Cook and Alexander Wedderburn, III, London, 1903, p. 624.

49. See Allen Staley, *The Pre-Raphaelite Landscape*, Oxford, 1973.

50. See Roger Smith, "Bonnard's Costume Historique—A Pre-Raphaelite Source Book," *Costume* 7 (1973), pp. 28-37; Stella Mary Newton, *Health, Art & Reason: Dress Reformers of the 19th Century*, London, 1974, ch. 2: "Pre-Raphaelite Clothing."

51. Hunt, 1905, I, pp. 130-31.

52. Ashton, 1980, p. iv.

53. Bevis Hillier, "The St. John's Wood Clique," *Apollo* 79 (1964), pp. 490-95.

54. Alan Hughes, *Henry Irving, Shakespearean*, Cambridge, 1981, pp. 158-59, compares Abbey's picture with Irving's staging of the scene, illustrating both; for a general discussion of Irving's relationships with artists, including Abbey, see Martin Meisel, *Realizations: Narrative, Pictorial, and Theatrical Arts in Nineteenth-Century England*, Princeton, 1983, ch. 19: "Irving and the Artists."

55. Abbey's costume sketches for Irving's *Richard II*, with attached fabric swatches, are now in the collection of the Yale University Art Gallery, New Haven, along with an extensive collection of his work received from his widow's estate.

56. See Cary M. Mazer, *Shakespeare Refashioned: Elizabethan Plays on Edwardian Stages*, Ann Arbor, 1981.

57. Quoted in Mrs. Russell Barrington, *The Life, Letters and Work of Frederick Leighton*, New York, 1906, II, p. 113.

58. "Chronicle of Art," *Magazine of Art* 11 (March 1888), p. xxii; Sadakichi Hartmann, *Shakespeare in Art*, Boston, 1901, pp. 86-89; the group of 21 *Graphic Heroines of Shakespeare*, each by a different artist, was sold at Christie's, London, March 9, 1889, under no. 299.

59. See Allen Staley, "The Condition of Music," *Art News Annual* 33 (1967), pp. 80-87; for a related development in the art of Millais, see Lucy Oakley, "The Evolution of Sir John Everett Millais's *Portia*," *Metropolitan Museum Journal* 16 (1981), pp. 181-94.

60. See Kenneth McConkey, "The Bouguereau of the Naturalists: Bastien Lepage and British Art," *Art History* 1 (1978), pp. 371-82; idem, "Listening to the Voices: A Study of Some Aspects of Jules Bastien-Lepage's 'Joan of Arc Listening to the Voices,'" *Arts Magazine* 56, no. 5 (January 1982), pp. 154-60.

61. See Anthea Callen, *Women Artists of the Arts and Crafts Movement, 1870-1914*, New York, 1979, ch. 3: "Embroidery and Needlework."

62. James Stanley Little, "Maurice Greiffenhagen and His Work," *Studio* 9 (1897), p. 239.

63. I am grateful to Professor Allen Staley of Columbia University for his encouragement, and for his comments on the manuscript, and to Katharine Baetjer of the Department of European Paintings, The Metropolitan Museum of Art, New York, for her interest and support.

Shakespeare and the Theatre of Illustration

By Cary M. Mazer

In 1899, the essayist and theatre critic Max Beerbohm attended a performance of a new production of Shakespeare's *King John* at Her Majesty's Theatre produced by his half brother, actor-manager Herbert Beerbohm Tree. The play was more familiar to Victorian audiences than it is to contemporary theatregoers; it had been regularly produced in the first half of the nineteenth century. But Beerbohm's contemporaries had only a few opportunities to see the play before (in 1865, 1873 and 1889), and so he did not assume that his readers had any greater familiarity with the play than he did. His review is not a mere plot summary, nor is it either an analysis of the actor's performances or a discussion of the treatment of the text. The review is, from first to last, a series of word-pictures.

Here, for example, is Beerbohm's description of the scene in which the King contemplates murdering the young Prince Arthur, the pretender to the throne who is in his custody:

> In a glade of slim beeches, John communes with the faithful, grim Hubert. The old soldier stands immovable, while his master whispers in his ear. Beyond, stands the queen mother, watching with her eyes of ill omen. Little Arthur is plucking the daisies. The king smiles down at him as he passes, and the child starts away. There are some daisies growing near the spot where the king has been whispering his behest. Lightly, he cuts the heads off them with his sword.[1]

Later, John believes that Hubert has carried out his secret command, but under new pressure from the Barons, he begins to regret the decision. Here is the description of the scene which follows in the production:

> All the vassals have left their king. The jester who watched the scene from a gallery has fled too. The king takes up the orb and the sceptre, sits haggard upon his throne. Hubert comes in, and the sound of his footstep causes the king to shudder and cry out like a child. But Arthur still lives. Nothing but his death-warrant remains against the king. While the king burns this parchment on the cresset, the monks file in to their Mass. Up the stairs they go, chanting. The king smiles, and then, still standing by the cresset, folds his hands in prayer. He walks, with bowed head, up the stairs, abases himself at the altar.

And here is Beerbohm's description of the final scene of the play, in which John dies, poisoned at the hand of papal spies:

> It is the dusk of dawn in the orchard of Swinstead Abbey, and through the apple-trees the monks hurry noiselessly to the chapel. The dying king is borne out in a chair. He is murmuring snatches of a song. The chair is set down, and with weak hands he motions away his bearers. 'Ay, marry,' he gasps, 'now my soul hath elbow-room; it would not out at windows nor at doors. There is so hot a summer in my bosom, that all my bowels crumble up to dust. . . . And none of you will bid the winter come, to thrust his icy fingers in my maw.' The bastard comes in hot haste, and the king, to receive his tidings, sits upright, and is crowned for the last time. He makes no answer to the tidings. One of the courtiers touches him, ever so lightly, on the shoulder, and he falls back. The crown is taken from his head and laid on the head of the child who is now king. The bastard rings out those words in which poetry of patriotism finds the noblest expression it can ever find.

Beerbohm's somewhat telegraphic descriptions of the fleeting impressions of the production vividly illustrate a particular sensibility on the part of the theatregoer and the producer of Shakespeare in the nineteenth century. The nineteenth-century theatre was the theatre of the star actor, presenting, on both sides of the Atlantic, successive generations of great and not-so-great performers such as John Philip Kemble and Sarah Siddons, Edmund Kean, William Charles Macready, Helen Faucit, Edwin Forrest, Charlotte Cushman, Charles Kean, Samuel Phelps, Edwin Booth, Henry Irving and Ellen Terry. But the actors and their actual performances are absent from Beerbohm's review. What we read instead is a description of a series of animated pictures in which the actors form only one part of the composition. Beerbohm paints a word-picture of the play in much the same way that he does for well-known paintings in his series of essays entitled "words for pictures." Beerbohm's words might almost be a prose paraphrase of the play in the style of Charles and Mary Lamb's *Tales from Shakespeare*; the lines of dialogue quoted might almost serve as captions to engravings illustrating the text.[2]

Note the details of the production that Beerbohm chooses to describe. Each scene is complete in its environmental details: the glade of beeches, which stand in contrast to the scene of assignation and contracting for murder taking place before them; the cresset in the throne room in which John burns the death sentence, echoing a cresset in an earlier scene, in which Hubert heats the pokers with which he plans to blind Arthur; and the glade of apple trees and the open air which provide the setting for John's death and the bastard Faulconbridge's final speech. Here too are characters, groupings, processions and ceremonies filling the canvas, helping to create the dramatic moment and to focus the viewer's attention on the silent thoughts of the character in the foreground: the jester silently commenting on the action, Elinor's hovering presence, the procession of monks creating a backdrop for John's silent destruction of the death warrant and his hypocritical prayer, and setting the scene for his death, poisoned by one of their number. A few of the effects are Shakespeare's own; but many of the effects are non- or extra-textual, adding to Shakespeare's bare lines to create effects which are perhaps more vivid, and certainly more elaborate, than Shakespeare's own. The burning of the death warrant, for example, is purely Tree's invention. Occasionally, the effects actually replace Shakespeare's words. For example, in the text, John tells Hubert to kill Arthur in a justifiably famous passage of stichomythia:

King John: Death.
Hubert: My lord.
King John: A grave.
Hubert: He shall not live.
King John: Enough.

Instead, in Tree's production, the king silently decapitates some daisies, in the garden in which Arthur has just been playing, with his sword. These are scenes from a theatre of pictorial composition and visual effect, a theatre of illustration. The scenic artist and the stage manager, like the painter of Shakespearean scenes and subjects, distills the dramatic moment into elaborate and eloquent, informationally dense, and aesthetically beautiful *pictures*.

This production by Beerbohm Tree, at the very end of the century, is indicative of a style, an idiom, perhaps even a discreet language of theatrical performance and production which emerged at the end of the eighteenth century and matured and flourished throughout the nineteenth, culminating in the art of Henry Irving in the 1880s and 90s, and declining somewhat into excess in the art of Beerbohm Tree. We can conveniently call this language of staging "pictorial realism." It is a theatre of illusion, of spectacle, of picture, of geographical and historical specificity. It is the theatre of the scene painter as well as the theatre of the star actor. And it is a theatre of an aesthetic that has a direct kinship with the art of the easel painter and book illustrator, the art represented in the present exhibition.

This was not the theatre for which Shakespeare wrote his plays. Shakespeare's theatre—the theatre of the reigns of Elizabeth I, James I and, after his death, Charles I, before the theatres were closed by the Puritans in 1642— was an open-air auditorium with an open stage, surrounded by the audience on three sides, with a neutral architectural facade behind. Shakespeare employed elaborate costumes, processions, sword-fights, special machine effects, significant gestures and symbolic actions. But his was not a theatre of *pictorial* illusion. No attempt was made to transform the visual appearance of the playing space to create a picture of an actual location; the players set the action of the scene and created a sense of actuality. By contrast, the theatre of the late eighteenth and nineteenth centuries, the theatre of pictorial realism, created an illusion of an actual place and time. The proscenium arch, behind which the action took place, was like a picture frame setting off a pictorial composition, or a window through which the audience viewed an illusionary world.

The theatre of pictorial realism has not, until fairly recently, received much scholarly respect. The neglect is partly the result of the "Shakespeare Revolution" that began at the end of the nineteenth century which fully swept away the old order by the years following the first World War.[3] Scholars and theatrical practioners alike were rediscovering the original stagecraft and dramaturgy of Shakespeare's plays which had been so distorted in the theatre of pictorial realism. The twentieth century invented, or reinvented, a theatre of convention rather than pictorial illusion, of suggestion rather than statement, of presentation rather than representation. The discovery of Shakespeare's Shakespeare has thrown the extravagant, spectacular theatre of the nineteenth century into eclipse. Only recently has the theatre of visual effect, the theatre of pictorial realism, been considered seriously, not for its failures to serve Shakespeare on his terms, but for its success in creating a coherent and effective aesthetic of its own.[4] What has emerged is a picture of an art form that shares a great number of aesthetic principles with the other aesthetic forms of the time, particularly painting.

The Painter in the Theatre

The more superficial points of contact between painting and the theatre in the late eighteenth and nineteenth centuries are many. Leading artists painted leading actors and actresses in and out of character: Reynolds, Hogarth, Zoffany and many others did portraits of David Garrick; Gainsborough and Reynolds painted Sarah Siddons, the latter choosing to represent her as the tragic muse herself; Lawrence painted Mrs. Siddons's brother, John Philip Kemble, as Hamlet; Whistler and Bastien-Lepage painted Henry Irving; Ellen Terry was painted by her first husband, G. F. Watts, and much later Sargent painted her as Lady Macbeth. Leading actors and managers enticed artists to work for them in the theatre: Garrick invited Philippe Jacques de Loutherbourg, newly arrived in London, to design scenes for his new productions at Drury Lane; the Bancrofts invited E.W. Godwin to advise them on the architecture and costumes for their 1875 revival of *The*

Merchant of Venice; and Irving employed Burne-Jones to design costumes and armor for his production of *King Arthur* (by Comyns Carr, after Mallory via Tennyson), Ford Madox Brown to provide a series of pictures for *King Lear*, and Lawrence Alma-Tadema to design scenery for *Coriolanus*, as did Tree for *Julius Caesar* and *Antony and Cleopatra*. Artists from de Loutherbourg through Godwin and Hubert Herkomer presented quasi-theatrical spectacular displays and private theatricals, experimenting with ways of perfecting the "optics" of stage illusion. The "Art of the Theatre" was regularly reported in *The Magazine of Art* and elsewhere, and many noted scene painters, such as Clarkson Stanfield, the Grieve family, William Telbin, Hawes Craven, and Joseph Harker received some degree of independent recognition in the artistic community for their work in the theatre.

Scenic design was primarily a painter's medium, even when scenery became increasingly three-dimensional and architectural. Painters were largely responsible for the continued impulse to perfect the illusion of reality in painting and in the theatre. De Loutherbourg displayed his "Eidophusikon" in 1781. This was an eight-foot wide by six-foot high miniature proscenium theatre, which created, through the art of the scene-painter, spectacular illusionistic vistas of exotic locations, natural disasters, and spectacular fictional cataclysms. Other spectacular exhibitions, such as panoramas, dioramas, magic lantern shows, and "dissolving views" (magic lantern displays in which one image would fade into the next), followed in the first few decades of the nineteenth century.[5] A number of these technical innovations were adapted for the theatre.

From the reopening of the theatres in 1660 through the mid-eighteenth century, painted scenery was largely a backdrop to the action played out on the apron stage in front of the proscenium; later, the apron dwindled, the action receded into the scenic space, and scenery served as a context, rather than a backdrop, for the action.[6] De Loutherbourg broke up the stage floor with ground rows extending from the wings, introducing asymmetry into the composition and creating a greater illusion of depth; and he introduced colored lighting in an attempt to create dramatic and "natural" effects. In the nineteenth century, candles and oil lamps were eventually replaced by gas lighting, which could be isolated, colored, and controlled more precisely.[7]

Throughout the century, scenery incorporated increasingly complex "set" pieces and "practical" units such as rostra, bridges, stairs, and facades of buildings to give the scene a greater sense of solidity. But even as the carpenter became more important, the scene painters retained their prominence. Three-dimensional units were constructed with various planes of painted scenery, and effects of surface texture, light and shadow continued to be created via painted effects (fig. 1). Examine, as just one example, the "heavy" scene from Edwin Booth's *Hamlet* of 1873 (fig. 2): the staircases and upstage rostrum

1. A scene of a building on fire viewed a) from the auditorium and b) from behind the scenes, From M. J. Moynet, *L'Envers du Theatre* (Paris: Librarie Hachette, 1888).

are practical; but the wall surfaces are created with painted canvas, and the colonnade at the top of the stairs is obviously a painted cut-cloth. Productions which employed "built-up" scenery still depended upon *trompe l'oeil* scene painting. Since built-up settings required time to set up, a "full" scene would have to be altered with a "front" scene, played downstage before a painted backdrop, often called "carpenter" scenes because they enabled the carpenters to change the built-up scenes behind them. Many of the drop cloths for these front scenes created extraordinary *trompe l'oeil* illusions through the scene painter's art. See, for example, Alma-Tadema's front scene of the exterior of Aufidius's house in Antium which he designed in the 1880s and executed in 1901 for

2. The play scene from Edwin Booth's *Hamlet*, McVicker's Theatre, Chicago, 1873 (Harvard Theatre Collection). With several shifting points of focus (primarily Hamlet, Claudius, and the Players), this is always a problematic scene to stage in a proscenium theatre. Compare Booth's solution to Daniel Maclise's in his painting, *The Play Scene from 'Hamlet'* (cat. no. 40), in which the frame of the painting creates a proscenium, and the play-within-a-play is staged on a proscenium-within-a-proscenium.

Irving's *Coriolanus*, a scene which Ellen Terry singles out as one of the most beautiful and effective front scenes in Irving's productions (fig. 3).[8]

Producers often cut and rearranged Shakespeare's plays in order to accommodate as few scene changes as possible. But even when producers were able to limit an entire act to a single heavy set, the scene would be preceded and followed by the lowering of an "act-drop," a front cloth painted with an elaborate vista or emblematic scene. Act-drops were often unrelated to the action of a particular play, but they were occasionally designed to fit a particular production, and provided an ongoing travelogue of the play's location, or a pictorial commentary on the action. For example, in Bancrofts' 1875 *The Merchant of Venice*, the act-drops presented other views of Venice from those offered in the action of the play.

For all the attempts to create an illusion of reality in the stage decor, the realism of the performance itself would be mitigated by frequent "tableaux," moments in which the action would freeze into an immobile picture, lasting anywhere from a fleeting moment to a half a minute or more. Tableaux often appeared at the beginning or middle of scenes, but most often came at their conclusion, and could be repeated or advanced, in stop-action, with each fall and rise of the "tableau" curtains. In the tableau, the art of the theatre would converge with the art of the gallery painter, for the entire resources of the stage, including the living actor, would imitate the immobile frozen moment captured in painting. The tableau was, as we will see, significant in relation to the theatre's strategy and techniques of story-telling, in ways which share many features with the techniques of narrative painting. But the tableau's closest affinity with contemporary painting lay in its actual imagery, for tableaux often consciously recreated popular paintings, engravings or book illustrations. This type of tableau was called a "realization." Such realizations of recognizable visual models were one of the theatre's principal means of creating effects. Plays were often conceived, and plots manufactured, strictly for the purpose of setting up a tableau realization, for example, of Wilkie's *Rent Day*, Gericault's *The Raft of the Medusa*, David's paintings of Napoleon, Delarouche's *Cromwell and Charles I*, or Frith's *Derby Day*; and novels such as Ainsworth's *Jack Sheppard* and the works of Dickens would be staged as a vehicle for the realization of the illustrations. Series of engravings, such as Hogarth's *The Harlot's Progress* and Cruikshank's *The Bottle*, were dramatized in order to realize the images in sequence.

Martin Meisel recently has shown at great length how these tableau realizations of visual material represent a convergence of the aesthetics of narrative painting, serial illustrated fiction, and the theatre in the nineteenth century.[9] According to Meisel, the three art forms (painting, fiction and the theatre) shared complementary sets of concerns: painting in capturing the fluidity of drama and the dimension of time in a single frozen image; fiction in painting dramatic scenes through both words and illustrations; and theatre in creating vivid pictorial effects.

There is no question that theatre artists in the nineteenth century drew upon the inspiration of paintings in their productions of Shakespeare's plays. In many cases, this was the result of a shared iconography, such as W. Moelwyn Merchant has shown was in effect in the depiction of the Act V Volumnia persuasion scene in *Coriolanus*, which drew its inspiration for visual realization in the theatre from Poussin.[10] Henry Irving's *King Lear* (1892) ultimately may have drawn upon Ford Madox Brown's two well-known paintings of scenes from the play, *Cordelia's Portion* (1866) and *Lear and Cordelia* (1948-49), than it did upon the sketches that

Brown prepared specifically for the production. Irving "realized" Edwin Abbey's *Richard, Duke of Gloucester, and the Lady Anne* (1896) when he restaged *Richard III* that same year. And Alma-Tadema was asked by Irving to incorporate a realization of Gérôme's *The Death of Ceasar* into a proposed (and ultimately unproduced) revival of *Julius Caesar*.

While nineteenth-century Shakespeare productions abounded in tableau scene endings and interpolated spectacles, they were generally less prone to outright realization than contemporary romantic and domestic melodramas and "sensation" plays. The real kinship between Shakespearean staging and paintings of Shakespearean subjects lies, not in the imitation or realization of specific paintings, nor in the employment of painters as scene designers and scene painters, but in a shared relationship to the literary source material.

The Theatre of Illustration

By the middle of the eighteenth century, Shakespeare's plays generally were regarded as the crowning achievement in English literature; and, since the Restoration, Shakespeare was the playwright whose works were most often performed in the commercial theatre. But these two facts are by no means directly interrelated. In the nineteenth century, the world of serious letters and the world of the professional theatre were almost unbridgeably separated. Except for notable cases of such major and minor literary figures as Lord Byron, Edward Bulwer-Lytton and Charles Reade, who wrote successful plays, and Dickens, who loved the theatre as an impassioned amateur, very few writers and artists occupied both worlds. Many noted literary critics, from Samuel Johnson through Charles Lamb, patronized and condescended to the performance of Shakespeare's plays in the theatre, preferring to read the plays and imagine the characters in the privacy of their studies to seeing them enacted, and inevitably limited, by the fleshy presence of the actor on the stage of the public playhouse. For all of the portraits of actors in their roles and paintings of scenes from their productions, the vast majority of paintings on Shakespearean subjects were not based on the Shakespeare of the theatre, but on the Shakespeare of the study, the Shakespeare of the literary critics and the paraphrasers, the Shakespeare of the expurgated illustrated *de luxe* family edition.

But this does not completely negate the connection between the visual arts and stage practice in nineteenth-century Shakespearean production. The relationship is less a matter of mutual influence than of shared source material. The key lies in the distinction that Meisel draws between the nineteenth-century definitions of "realization" and "illustration."[11] Realization is a translation from one medium to another, adding, for example, the third dimension of the actor and the scenic space to the two dimensions of the canvas. Illustration, on the other hand, is a form of amplification, or elaboration, a gloss or commentary on the source material, rather than an exact fulfillment of it. From Boydell and his Shakespeare Gallery onwards, Shakespearean painting was Shakespearean illustration. Similarly, the theatre of pictorial realism in the nineteenth century was, with regard to Shakespeare production at least, a theatre of illustration. Performance of the plays upon the stage was a means of commenting upon and of embellishing the literary source material; of telling the stories, in the language of living pictures, that the dramatist told in his plays; and of presenting a proscenium-sized illustrated textbook on the history, geography and culture of the

3. The Exterior of Aufidius' house in Antium, designed by Lawrence Alma-Tadema for Henry Irving's production of *Coriolanus*, Lyceum Theatre, 1901 (from *The Architectural Review*, 1901).

4. Four antiquarian costume designs for Shakespeare productions at Covent Garden, 1824-25: a) King John, b) a courtier in *As You Like It*, c) Hamlet, and d) Othello (Furness Collection, University of Pennsylvania).

worlds in which the plays are set. Many Shakespearean actors and producers in the nineteenth century, fighting centuries of prejudice against their art and profession, used Shakespeare's plays as a means of elevating their art into the ranks of high culture: Macready, with his stinging sense of the actor's partly justified low social status; Charles Kean, turning the plays into elaborately footnoted historical pageants to be performed, along with "gentlemanly melodrama," for his carriage-trade audiences at the Princess's Theatre; Samuel Phelps, playing Shakespeare to the working-class audiences of Islington at the Sadler's Wells Theatre; and Henry Irving, turning the Lyceum Theatre into a temple of high culture, the de facto "House of Shakespeare," and earning for himself a knighthood. All of these theatre artists were not so much performing Shakespeare's plays, but rather illustrating, with all the histrionic and scenic resources at their command, the Shakespeare of the *de luxe* family edition. Like prose paraphrases, Shakespearean "galleries," and operatic or balletic adaptations of the plays, stage productions of Shakespeare's plays in the nineteenth century were illustrations of literary source material, rather than fulfillments of the dramatist's own theatrical demands or expectations.

The features that Shakespearean painting and Shakespearean performance of the nineteenth century have in common, then, are not so much the product of their interrelationship as of their parallel relationship to literary, rather than theatrical, sources. And so we return to Max Beerbohm's description of Tree's production of *King John*, more a series of elaborately detailed, animated pictures from Shakespeare's story than a staging of Shakespeare's play. Like painting, the stage of that period was primarily a visual medium. The stage, like the canvas, was frontal, framed, illusionistic, and painterly. And each medium, equally concerned with the illustration of the literary source material, employed a similar strategy of contextualization and narrative exposition.

The Worlds of the Plays: History, Culture, Context

The Boydell Shakespeare Gallery and the rise in historical painting was reflected in, and to a certain extent directly influenced, a new sense of history and historicism in Shakespearean staging. Through the mid-eighteenth century, history was presented in a more generalized manner on the stage: plumes, helmets and breastplates might be exotic, but the basic features of the costumes were contemporary with the theatre audience. But now, with the action taking place amidst the scenery and behind the proscenium arch, context becomes as important as action. Shakespeare's Romans, Renaissance Italians, and Lancastrian Englishmen were then believed to be distinct from one another and from people in the present, in dress and behavior if not in their fundamental, "universal" human emotions. This was, of course, the era of Romanticism, of Walter Scott and the historical novel. It was generally held that if Shakespeare had failed to show the worlds which his characters inhabit, it was because his theatre did not have the resources to do so; he nevertheless did have a picture of these worlds, countries, cultures and epochs in mind when he wrote his plays, and it was the modern theatrical artist's responsibility to represent these worlds in the stage picture.[12]

Othello
1st Dress

As early as the 1790s, William Capon's designs for Shakespeare's history plays for John Philip Kemble at Covent Garden depicted historically accurate architectural features. By 1823, historicism was in full swing in Shakespearean production when Kemble's younger brother Charles staged *King John* at Covent Garden with J. R. Planché in charge of antiquarian details. Planché, a playwright and opera librettist, as well as a designer and antiquarian, published his designs for the Covent Garden revivals, and in 1834 published one of the first and most comprehensive textbooks on historical costume (fig. 4). Planché continued to work in this line, assisting Madame Vestris with her spectacular production of *A Midsummer Night's Dream* in 1840, and Macready with his series of revivals at Drury Lane from 1837 to 1843.[13] From these productions onward, Shakespearean producers were unabashed in their claims to historicism, antiquarianism, and "archaeological" accuracy, both for the sake of theatrical effect, and in order to promote the educational benefits of theatregoing.

The most grand of the antiquarians was Charles Kean, who produced a series of Shakespearean productions at the Princess's Theatre in the 1850s. Kean's printed programs featured elaborate essays on the documentary sources for the costumes, sets and properties: a little toy wagon drawn on by the young Mamilius in *The Winter's Tale* (1856) was credited to an object in the British Museum. (A contemporary burlesque of the production claimed the bear in Act III was copied from the original in Noah's ark.) *The Winter's Tale* is a hodgepodge of historical periods and cultures: Sicilia in the age of the Delphic oracle, with a queen whose father is the emperor of Russia; and Bohemia, with an inaccurate sea-coast, with sheep-shearing festivals and peasant rustics out of Shakespeare's own contemporary Warwickshire. Appalled by such inconsistencies, Kean set Sicilia as Syracusa of the classical period, and emended Bohemia to Bythinia of the same historical era.[14] In 1857, during the long run of his spectacular revival of *Richard II*, Kean was made a Fellow of the Society of Antiquarians.

Another noted antiquarian working in the theatre was the architect and designer E. W. Godwin, who published a series of essays in *The Architect* on "The Architecture and Costume of Shakespeare's Plays." In these essays, Godwin advises strict historical accuracy in costume, with some allowances made for Shakespeare's often shaky conception of the period in question. The scenes are conceived architecturally and in three dimensions, and are based on real rooms, streets and locations in the cities in which Shakespeare sets the action (fig. 5). The extent of Godwin's actual contribution to the 1875 production of *The Merchant of Venice* at the Prince of Wales's Theatre is subject to some debate, but it is clear that his participation reflected, if not influenced, the attention to three-dimensional architectural detail and to geographic and historical specificity of costume and customs.[15]

The theatre of pictorial realism, then, shared with historical painting a concern for a strict accuracy of visual detail. Therefore, it was only natural that the painters who specialized in particular historical periods would be called upon to serve as advisors and designers for plays set in that period; Alma-Tadema was the natural choice for any Victorian or Edwardian actor-manager wishing to stage Shakespeare's Roman plays. But, as in historical painting, archaeological detail was not merely an end in itself, but a means of telling a story, of creating a context for the dramatic action. Productions of *The Merchant of Venice* presented not only views of the canals and buildings of Venice, but introduced elaborate pantomime sequences of the teeming life of the city to create a context for the action of the play. The Padua of *The Taming of the Shrew* and the Messina of *Much Ado About Nothing* were shown in accurate detail, based on meticulous drawings sketched on location by scene designers sent abroad for the purpose, because it was believed that the Italian climate and culture were appropriate to the frolicksome comedy in the plays; and the sun-baked days and sultry evenings of Renaissance Verona were believed to be of particular relevance to the hot-blooded passions of feuding, love and death in *Romeo and Juliet*. (See, for example, Hawes Craven's lyrical setting for the balcony scene of Forbes Robertson's 1895 production of the play, fig. 6.)

Even plays with historical settings were subject to the same contextual scrutiny. On Ford Madox Brown's advice, for example, Irving decided to set *King Lear*, according to his program note, in "a time shortly after the departure of the Romans, when the Britons would naturally inhabit the houses left vacant." This provided both a

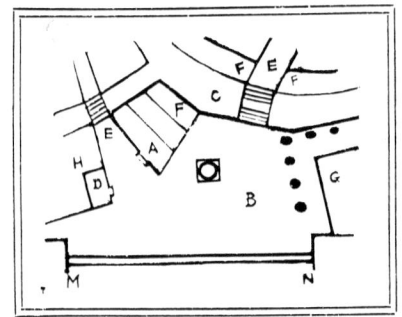 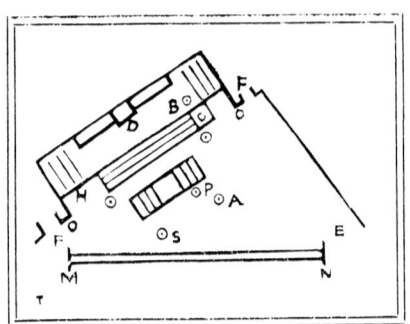 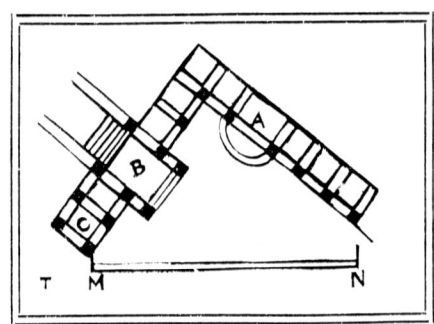

5. Three ground plans for *The Merchant of Venice* by E.W. Godwin, from "The Architecture and Costume of Shakespeare's Plays" (1874): a) a public place in Venice (A is Shylock's house, C is a canal, and M-N is the proscenium; b) the court of justice; and c) Belmont (the caskets are placed at A).

political explanation and a visual metaphor for the pathos of the drama. The sense of a crumbling civilization which had lost its rationale, of violence beneath the surface, of power wrested or bartered away, were all conveyed through the overgrown vines engulfing the crumbling architecture of an imported higher civilization. The play ends beneath the natural immensity of the chalk cliffs at Dover, which fill the entire backdrop of the final scene (fig. 7). These cliffs lend a similar presence to Edward Matthew Ward's *King Lear and Cordelia* (cat. no. 62) where they make a more dramatic statement than they do in Brown's painting of the same subject. Irving was particularly fond of creating visual images of foreboding tragedy. At least one scene in each of his productions of Shakespearean tragedies would feature a large, threatening tree, which visually symbolized the power of fate; Alma-Tadema's front scene for *Coriolanus* (fig. 3) shows the "fate tree" in that production.

The specific choice of location for the action of the scenes was as important as the general accuracy of period and place. Scenes could be shifted from public to private spaces, from indoors to outdoors, to suit the particular emotional and dramatic qualities which the actor-manager and scenic artist wish to convey. Frederick Richard Pickersgill sets his painting of *Viola and the Countess* from *Twelfth Night* (cat. no. 50), presumably a depiction of either III, i or III, iv, in Olivia's garden, in keeping with the dramatic demands of the scene. But it was not unusual for producers to set virtually the entire play in Olivia's garden, making the set for that location the single "heavy" scene of the production, and playing all other scenes as front scenes. Hawes Craven's elaborate setting for Beerbohm Tree's production was copied from an illustration in *Country Life* (fig. 8). In Augustin Daly's production of the play in New York and London, the use of the garden setting created several problems of logic: when Malvolio hurries after Viola to give her Olivia's ring, he finds her in precisely the place he last saw her when she made her exit from the preceding scene. And producers could depart from tradition in their placement of key scenes. Forbes Robertson, for example, modified the traditional visual tone of Hamlet's long encounter with the Ghost on the battlements by setting the scene instead on a beach.

Shakespeare occasionally established, though through non-pictorial means, a relationship, often a contrasting one, between dramatic action and the locality in which it unfolds: a ceremony will be interrupted, or an anomalous presence in black will be seen in the middle of a festively dressed court. Such scenes were suited perfectly for the

6. Hawes Craven's rendering of the balcony scene for Forbes Robertson's *Romeo and Juliet*, Lyceum Theatre, 1895, as printed along with the souvenir script of the production (London: The Nassau Press, 1895).

7. Hawes Craven's rendering of the final scene in Henry Irving's *King Lear*, Lyceum Theatre, 1892 (Shakespeare Centre Library, Stratford-upon-Avon).

theatre of pictorial realism, with its enormous capacity for pageantry and elaborate setting. This was not so with Shakespeare's scheme for the graveyard scene in Hamlet: rarely did Victorian producers choose to show Ophelia's funeral as "maimed rites" when they could easily bring on as many priests, nuns and pall-bearers as they could muster and clothe. But the church scene (IV, i) in *Much Ado About Nothing* is more typical. In Shakespeare's play, the marriage ceremony between Claudio and Hero is interrupted when Claudio falsely accuses his bride of wantonness. The towering architecture of the church (often copied directly from the cathedral in Messina), the festive costumes, the religious trappings and the organ music all set the scene and establish a ceremonial event which will be violated. The deliberate dramatic contrast between action and setting is evident in Alfred W. Elmore's painting of the scene (cat. no. 21). It is even more apparent in a painting by the artist-turned-actor, Johnston Forbes Robertson, of the scene as staged in Henry Irving's 1882 production of the play (fig. 9). Forbes Robertson, more interested in creating accurate portraits of the actors in their roles (including a self-portrait in the role of Claudio), does not convey the dramatic action as successfully as Elmore, but he does convey the sense of grandeur achieved in the elaborate sets and the management of the stage crowds. While Victorian theatre artists were successful in staging Claudio's breech of decorum in his rejection of Hero at the altar, they were less comfortable with the episode that follows, in which Beatrice commands Benedick to take revenge, a scene which seemed to them to be too indecorous for a church; Tree solved this problem, or what was perceived to be a problem, by splitting the scene in two, and shifting the latter half of the scene to an adjoining cloisters.

The visual specificity of the theatre of pictorial realism enabled the theatrical producer and the scenic artist to create a complete picture of the world of the play. In the theatre of illustration, as in historical painting, historical, cultural and environmental details were not merely ends in themselves, but the means of creating a sense of context for the dramas unfolding within those worlds.

Illustration and Narrative

Pictorial realism was not only a means of establishing a context for the drama; it was a pictorial means of story-telling, of carrying forward the narrative energies of the illustrated theatrical edition of the play. If Shakespeare's story was based on familiar history, then a pictorial interpolation might illustrate episodes from history which Shakespeare chose not to dramatize, but which were important events in the audience's understanding of the story. Max Beerbohm failed to mention that Tree's *King John* included a tableau depiction of the signing of the Magna Carta at Runymede, an event which every school-child associates with the reign of King John, but which has no bearing on the main action of Shakespeare's play. Charles Kean included in Act V of *Henry VIII* in 1855 a moving panorama of the barge ride from London to Greenwich Palace where the christening of Princess Elizabeth in the final scene was to take place: the view from the river of each location en route passed across the stage, unrolling from an immense spool on one side of the stage and rolling onto another at the other side. The "Panorama," a popular form of spectacular display in exhibition halls, had already been incorporated into pantomimes and melodramas; here, it serves as a device for theatrical story-telling.

Episodes which Shakespeare describes through the mouths of his characters but does not show the audience were frequently staged. Charles Kean's *Richard II* (1857) included an elaborate staging of Richard's and Boling-broke's entries into London, an episode narrated by the Duke of York in V, ii. Such an approach to the plays corresponds to those of contemporary painters and prose paraphrasers of the plays. The most famous example in

8. Charles Buchel's rendering of Hawes Craven's design for the garden scene in Beerbohm Tree's *Twelfth Night*, Her Majesty's Theatre, 1901 (Beerbohm Tree Collection, University of Bristol Theatre Collection). In the actual set, only the first two tiers of grassy steps were practical; the rest (including the step on which Buchel places Malvolio) were painted *trompe l'oiel*.

Victorian painting is, of course, Millais's depiction of the drowning of Ophelia, an episode described in the play by Gertrude in IV, vii. Laurence Olivier, exploiting the pictorial capabilities of the film in his version of *Hamlet* in 1948, chose to realize this painting, with Gertrude's speech as a voice-over.

The narrative function of stage pictorialism, like contemporary narrative painting, carried with it the aesthetic assumption that the lives and worlds of the characters were not confined to the relatively narrow time scheme dramatized by Shakespeare in the play itself. An extreme example in painting is Calderon's *The Young Lord Hamlet* (cat. no. 9), which "illustrates" a passage in Hamlet's recollection of Yorick while contemplating the jester's unearthed skull in the graveyard: "He hath bore me on his back a thousand times, and now how abhorred in my imagination it is!" Calderon eliminates any allusion to mortality and putrescence, except perhaps for the gargoyles on the wall, and shows us a youthful idyll, including not only the young Hamlet, with a playful puppy providing symbolic commentary on the carefree frivolity of youth, but the infant Ophelia looking on, and reaching out from the sidelines toward the main action, as she so often does in the play. Calderon's visual extension of the lives of the characters into the years preceding the action of the play parallels that of Mary Cowden Clarke, whose *The Girlhood of Shakespeare's Heroines*, while making no claims towards delimiting or defining the characters as they actually appear in the plays, does provide edifying accounts of the characters in their childhood, elaborating upon telltale references in the plays about the characters and their earlier relationships, in much the same way that Calderon foreshadows the relationship between Hamlet and Ophelia. In a similar vein is Calderon's depiction of Angelo's rejection of Mariana in *Measure for Measure*. Calderon chooses a two-character scene which is only indirectly narrated in the play, rather than confrontations actually dramatized in the play, between Angelo and Isabella, or between Isabella and her brother Claudio in prison, a subject treated by Holman Hunt and others.[16] Angelo's relationship with Mariana has come to an end well before the action of the play begins; Mariana does not appear in the play until IV, i; and her very existence, let alone her previous relationship with Angelo, is not even mentioned until the end of III, i, after virtually all of Angelo's major appearances in the play. Calderon's depiction of Angelo's rejection of Mariana, which he sets in a garden suggestive of the "moated grange" in which Mariana later resides, serves not only as a narrative interpolation preceding the action of the play, but as footnote to Angelo's character, showing us a degree of open emotional expression which the character does not demonstrate during the course of the play itself.

In the theatre, the major device used to illustrate the lives of the characters beyond the events dramatized by the playwright was the tableau. As we have seen, the tableau was often a frozen image, realizing a popular painting or book illustration. But tableaux could also be elaborate, animated, pantomime sequences, extending the action of the play beyond the fictional time allotted to the spoken words of the text. Such episodes would occasionally be placed after the curtain would fall at the end of a scene; the curtains would rise again, showing the characters and the dramatic action after some interval of time, either a moment or several hours, had passed. Henry Irving, in his production of *The Merchant of Venice* in 1879, showed Shylock returning from dinner, some time after the Christian revelers had run off with his daughter Jessica, knocking on the door of his house which we know to be empty. The curtain falls again, leaving us to believe that the scene of discovery will

9. Johnston Forbes Robertson's painting of the church scene from Irving's *Much Ado About Nothing*, Lyceum Theatre, 1882 (The Players Club). Included in the painting are portraits of (l. to r.) Ellen Terry (Beatrice), James Fernandez (Leonato), Thomas Mead (Friar Francis), Jessie Millward (Hero), Forbes Robertson (Claudio), William Terris (Don Pedro), Henry Irving (Benedick), and Charles Glenney (Don John).

inevitably follow in the world of the play, even though the curtain will tastefully hide these events from our eyes. Tree, leaving less to the imagination, extending this tableau sequence further in his 1908 production of the play, showed Shylock searching the house in despair, and rending his clothing and throwing dirt upon his head in ritual mourning for his daughter.

The pictorial realism of the theatre creates a world with a life of its own behind the proscenium arch; the tableau interpolation creates the illusion that this world continues after the scene is over. In effect, the playwright, assisted by the actor-manager and the scene painter, occasionally raises the curtain to allow the audience sequential glimpses into the world of the play, a series of carefully composed pictures which together tell the story. The pictures that the theatre artist chooses to create are not always the ones employed by the dramatist. But, then again, serial pictorial story-telling was not Shakespeare's dramatic strategy in the first place. The story is Shakespeare's, but the story-teller is the actor, the stage manager, and the scene painter. And the language of story-telling in the theatre is unlike that of either Shakespeare's theatre or our own. It shares its basic vocabulary with the other pictorial arts of the nineteenth century: historical and narrative painting, and book illustration.

This essay began with Max Beerbohm's description of several scenes from a Shakespeare production by Beerbohm Tree. To close, here is Beerbohm's description of a single, non-textual moment from Tree's often-revived 1901 production of *Twelfth Night*. The scene is II, iii, here set, as it is traditionally, in the kitchen of Olivia's house. The verbal action of the scene is over: Sir Toby, Sir Andrew, Maria and Feste have roused the sleeping Malvolio with their caterwauling; Malvolio has reprimanded and threatened them; and, after he leaves, the midnight revelers have hatched a scheme to get even with him. At the end of this scene, Beerbohm writes,

"comes an effect which Shakespeare did not, perhaps, adumbrate in his stage directions, but which rounds it off very prettily":

> *As the two topers reel off to bed, the uncanny dawn peers at them through the windows. The Clown wanders on, humming a snatch of the tune he has sung to them. He looks at the empty bowl of sack and the overturned tankards, smiles, shrugs his shoulders, yawns, lies down before the embers of the fire, goes to sleep. Down the stairs, warily, with a night-cap on his head and a sword in his hand, comes Malvolio, awakened and fearful of danger. He peers around, lunging with his sword at the harmless furniture. One thinks of Don Quixote and 'the notable adventure of the wine-skins.' Satisfied, he retraces his footsteps up the staircase. A cock crows, and, as the curtain falls, one is aware of a whole slumbering household, and of the mystery of an actual dawn.*

The scene ends, then, not as it does in Shakespeare's play, but with an illustration, an illustration which might just as easily be found in a prose paraphrase of the play's story, or in an illustrated family edition of the play, a picture of an extended moment of time, depicting the life of the house and the people that live there in all its physical and temporal details, such as might be painted by a Royal Academician. Beerbohm's conclusion cautions us against judging the aesthetic success of such an illustration on the basis of its fidelity to Shakespeare's dramaturgy, a warning which may well apply to our own assessment of all nineteenth-century Shakespearean illustration, in the theatre and in the picture gallery:

> *Pedants may cavil at such imaginative glosses in a production of Shakespeare. To me, the question is simply whether the imagination be of a good or bad kind. In this instance the imagination seems to me distinctly good.*[17]

NOTES

1. Max Beerbohm, review first published 30 September 1899, reprinted in *More Theatres* (New York: Taplinger Publishing Company, 1969), pp. 191-192.

2. Beerbohm's description of IV, i is interesting in this context. This scene, in which Hubert sets out to blind and murder Arthur, only to be dissuaded by the young prince's eloquence, was one of the best-known scenes in the play, and by far the most widely illustrated. (There are two versions, by George Harlow and by James Northcote, in the Picture Gallery of the Royal Shakespeare Theatre in Stratford-upon-Avon.) Beerbohm writes only: "In the crypt there is no light but the cresset where the irons will be heated. Arthur runs in, carrying a cross-bow on his shoulder. 'Good morrow, Hubert.' 'Good morrow, little prince . . .'" He sets the scene and then says no more, confident that the reader will complete the picture according to the familiar pictorial iconography of painting and book-illustration.

3. This term was coined by J. L. Styan in *The Shakespeare Revolution: Criticism and Performance in the Twentieth Century* (Cambridge: Cambridge University Press, 1977).

4. Book length studies include Michael R. Booth, *Victorian Spectacular Theatre, 1850-1910* (Boston: Routledge and Kegan Paul, 1981), which includes a chapter on Shakespeare and a reconstruction of Tree's 1910 *Henry VIII*; Martin Meisel, *Realizations* (see note 9 below); Alan Hughes, *Henry Irving, Shakespearean* (Cambridge: Cambridge University Press, 1981); sections of George Rowell, *The Victorian Theatre, 1792-1914* (Cambridge: Cambridge University Press, second edition, 1978) and the second chapter of Rowell's *Theatre in the Age of Irving* (Totowa: Rowman and Littlefield, 1981); and Cary M. Mazer, *Shakespeare Refashioned: Elizabethan Plays on Edwardian Stages* (Ann Arbor: UMI Research Press, 1981). Recent articles on the stagecraft of Beerbohm Tree include John Ripley, "'Imagination Holds Dominion': Stage Spectacles in Beerbohm Tree's Productions, 1897-1900" (*Theatre Survey* 9 [1969] 11-20); Richard Foulkes, "Herbert Beerbohm Tree's *Henry VIII*: Expenditure, Spectacle and Experiment" (*Theatre Research International* 3 [1977] 22-32); Michael Mullin, "Strange Images of Death: Sir Herbert Beerbohm Tree's *Macbeth*" (*Theatre Survey* 17 [1976] 125-142); and Ralph Berry, "Beerbohm Tree as Director: Three Shakespeare Productions" (*Essays in Theatre* 1 [1983] 73-80). Russell Jackson, who has written on Victorian producers such as Edward Saker and Lewis Wingfield, is currently completing a book on Victorian Shakespeare productions for Cambridge University Press.

5. For an account of these and other spectacular exhibitions, see Richard D. Altick, *The Shows of London: A Panoramic History of Exhibitions, 1600-1862* (Cambridge: Harvard University Press, 1978).

6. For an excellent survey see Sybil Rosenfeld, *A Short History of Scene Design in Great Britain* (Oxford: Basil Blackwell, 1973) and her book-length expansion of one chapter of that book, *Georgian Scene Painters and Scene Painting* (Cambridge: Cambridge University Press, 1981).

7. See Terence Rees, *Theatre Lighting in the Age of Gas* (London: The Society for Theatre Research, 1978).

8. Ellen Terry, *The Story of My Life* (London: Hutchinson & Co., 1908), pp. 172-173.

9. Martin Meisel, *Realizations: Narrative, Pictorial and Dramatic Arts in Nineteenth-Century England* (Princeton: Princeton University Press, 1983). All of the examples in the preceding paragraph are drawn from Meisel's chapters on the "conjunctions" between the arts.

10. W. Moelwyn Merchant, *Shakespeare and the Artist* (London: Oxford University Press, 1959), pp. 178-189. Merchant's parallel history of Shakespearean painting and illustration and theatrical decor for Shakespearean production is still the standard text on the subject.

11. See Chapter 2, "Illustration and Realization" in Meisel, *Realizations*, pp. 29-37.

12. See Mazer, *Shakespeare Refashioned*, pp. 9-11. Theatre artists and critics often cited the first Chorus speech from Shakespeare's *Henry V* as proof that Shakespeare would have wanted to realize pictorially the locality of each scene's action, had his theatre had the means to do so. See Mazer, pp. 51-52, and Booth, *Victorian Spectacular Theatre*, pp. 30-32.

13. See Gary J. Williams, "Madame Vestris' *A Midsummer Night's Dream* and the Web of Victorian Tradition" (*Theatre Survey* 18 [1977] 1-22).

14. For a thorough, and only slightly condescending, account of Charles Kean's *The Winter's Tale*, see Dennis Bartholomeusz, *The Winter's Tale In Performance in England and America, 1611-1976* (Cambridge: Cambridge University Press, 1982), pp. 81-100.

15. For a contemporary scholarly account of Godwin's career in the theatre, see John Stokes, *Resistible Theatres: Enterprise and Experiment in the Late Nineteenth Century* (London: Paul Elek Books Ltd., 1972), pp. 31-68. Oscar Wilde has a lengthy appreciation of Godwin in "The Truth of Masks" (1891), reprinted in *The Artist as Critic*, ed. Richard Ellmann, (New York: Vintage Books, 1968), pp. 408-432.

16. For an account of Hunt's painting and the genre of prison scenes in painting and the theatre, see Chapter 14, "Prisoners Base," in Meisel, *Realizations*, pp. 283-301.

17. Beerbohm, 7 February 1901, *More Theatres*, p. 349.

Plate I
Edwin Austin Abbey
The Penance of Eleanor, Duchess of Gloucester, 1900
Museum of Art, The Carnegie Institute, Pittsburgh

Plate II
Washington Allston
Falstaff Enlisting His Ragged Regiment at Justice Shallow's, ca. 1806-08
Wadsworth Atheneum, Hartford, Gift from the existing Trustee of the Allston Trust.

Plate III
Philip Hermogenes Calderon
The Young Lord Hamlet, 1868
Mr. and Mrs. E. Hal Dickson, Mr. and Mrs. James R. Duncan, and Mr. and Mrs. Frank W. Rose, San Angelo, Texas

Plate IV
Alexandre-Marie Colin
The Three Witches from Macbeth, 1827
Mr. and Mrs. E. Hal Dickson, Mr. and Mrs. James R. Duncan,
and Mr. and Mrs. Frank W. Rose, San Angelo, Texas

Plate V
Richard Dadd
Titania Sleeping, ca. 1841
Peter Nahum, London

Plate VI
Walter Howell Deverell
Twelfth Night, 1850
The FORBES Magazine Collection, New York

Plate VII
Alfred W. Elmore
Much Ado About Nothing
Mr. and Mrs. E. Hal Dickson, Mr. and Mrs. James R. Duncan, and Mr. and Mrs. Frank W. Rose, San Angelo, Texas

Plate VIII
John Faed
Shakespeare and His Contemporaries
Mr. and Mrs. E. Hal Dickson, Mr. and Mrs. James R. Duncan,
and Mr. and Mrs. Frank W. Rose, San Angelo, Texas

Plate IX
Henry Fuseli
Lady Constance, Arthur, Salisbury, 1783
Smith College Museum of Art, Northampton, Massachusetts
Purchased with the Gift of Eleanor Lamont Cunningham

Plate X
Wladyslaw Von Czachorski
The Actors Before Hamlet, 1875
Mr. and Mrs. E. Hal Dickson, Mr. and Mrs. James R. Duncan,
and Mr. and Mrs. Frank W. Rose, San Angelo, Texas

Plate XI
John Gilbert
The Plays of William Shakespeare, 1849
Mr. and Mrs. E. Hal Dickson, Mr. and Mrs. James R. Duncan,
and Mr. and Mrs. Frank W. Rose, San Angelo, Texas

Plate XII
Maurice Greiffenhagen
Ophelia and Laertes, 1885
Mr. and Mrs. E. Hal Dickson, Mr. and Mrs. James R. Duncan, and Mr. and Mrs. Frank W. Rose, San Angelo, Texas

Plate XIII
Edward Robert Hughes
The Shrew Katherina, 1896
Mr. and Mrs. E. Hal Dickson, Mr. and Mrs. James R. Duncan,
and Mr. and Mrs. Frank W. Rose, San Angelo, Texas

Plate XIV
Henry Stacy Marks
Bardolph, 1853
Mr. and Mrs. E. Hal Dickson, Mr. and Mrs. James R. Duncan, and Mr. and Mrs. Frank W. Rose, San Angelo, Texas

Plate XV
Frederick Richard Pickersgill
Viola and the Countess, 1859
Mr. and Mrs. E. Hal Dickson, Mr. and Mrs. James R. Duncan,
and Mr. and Mrs. Frank W. Rose, San Angelo, Texas

Plate XVI
Paul Falconer Poole
A Scene From The Tempest, 1856
The Forbes Magazine Collection, New York

Plate XVII
Robert Smirke
Falstaff Examining Prince Hal
Bob Jones University, Greenville, South Carolina

Plate XVIII
Thomas Sully
George Frederick Cooke as Richard III, 1811
The Pennsylvania Academy of Fine Arts, Philadelphia,
Presented by Friends and Admirers of the Artist.

Plate XIX
Thomas Sully
Portia and Shylock, 1835
The Folger Shakespeare Library, Washington, D.C.

Catalogue of the Exhibition
By Margaret Lynne Ausfeld

ACKNOWLEDGMENTS

Many individuals have offered invaluable assistance, advice and encouragement in the preparation of the catalogue of paintings for *A Brush with Shakespeare: The Bard in Painting, 1789-1910*. I would like to thank each of those who gave so generously of their knowledge and time, including: Geoffrey Ashton, Librarian, The Garrick Club; Professor Kalman A. Burnim, Tufts University; Susan P. Casteras, Assistant Curator and Tom Hill, Librarian, The Yale Center for British Art; David J. Clarke, Curator, The Carlisle Museum; Hilarie Faberman, Curator, The University of Michigan Museum of Art; Paula B. Freedman, Yale University Art Gallery; John Goodwin, The National Theatre; Janet Griffin and Catherine Johnson, The Folger Shakespeare Library; A. V. Griffiths, The British Museum; Robin Hamlyn, The Tate Gallery; Patricia Jaffe, The Fitzwilliam Museum; Stephen Jones, Curator, Leighton House; Margaret Kelly, Curator, The Forbes Collection; Sally Mills, Curator, Vassar College Art Gallery; Peter Nahum, London; Louis A. Rachow, Curator and Librarian, The Players; Professor Robert Rosenblum, New York University; Julia Nell Rutledge, Montgomery Public Library; Allen Scott, Kurt Schon, Ltd.; Diana Strazdes, Carnegie Institute; Professor Richard R. Studing, Wayne State University; Wendy Warnken and Mary Ann Smith, Theatre Collection Museum of the City of New York. I am especially grateful to Lucy Oakley whose insightful suggestions and observations are incorporated throughout these entries.—M.L.A.

Catalogue Notes:

Measurements are given in inches, width precedes height. Abbreviations used are: N.A., **National Academy**; P.R.A., **President of the Royal Academy**; R.A., **Royal Academician**; R.S.A., **Royal Scottish Academy**; R.W.S., **Royal Watercolor Society**.

1
Edwin Austin Abbey, N.A., R.A.
American, 1852-1911
The Play Scene in 'Hamlet', 1897
Oil on canvas, 61¼ x 96½
Signed lower left: E. A. Abbey 1897
The Edwin Austin Abbey Memorial Collection,
Yale University Art Gallery, New Haven, Connecticut

In a presentation fraught with psychological drama, Edwin Austin Abbey has made the viewer a key element in his 1897 depiction of the play scene from *Hamlet* by placing an imaginary stage before the picture plane and within the viewer's space. This device, with its theatrical implications, demonstrates Abbey's appreciation of the parallel relationships in painting, theatre and literature which had flourished in the nineteenth century.[1] This awareness, combined with his historicism and fascination with the aesthetics of the Pre-Raphaelite Brotherhood, were significant in determining Abbey's approach.

One of the great illustrators and muralists of the American Renaissance period, Abbey attended the Pennsylvania Academy of the Fine Arts in his hometown of Philadelphia. Beginning his career in 1871 at the age of 19 as an illustrator for *Harper's* in New York, in 1878 Abbey went to London. There he won fame as an illustrator of English literary classics, including the plays of William Shakespeare. He remained in England, living and working in the Worcestershire hamlet of Broadway, a rural setting where his imaginative sense of history was nurtured. Swept up in the fashion for historical accuracy in art and the theatre, Abbey acquired a vast knowledge of English history, doing painstaking archaeological research and collecting costumes, furniture and architectural accessories to lend authenticity to his paintings and illustrations.[2]

As a student in Philadelphia, Abbey especially admired the works of D. G. Rossetti and the other Pre-Raphaelites. The psychological intensity with which they endowed literary subjects is also evident in Abbey's interpretation of *Hamlet*'s "play within a play." The episode had been previously depicted, most notably by Daniel Maclise in 1842. (See cat. no. 40.) Arranged compositionally in a manner which suggests a stage setting, the emphasis is nonetheless placed on characterization which provides a human dimension to the narrative. Moody, oppressive silence pervades his audience of Danish courtiers (who are genuine Celtic types in appropriate costume)[3] as they watch the "dumb show" Hamlet has orchestrated to recreate the murder of his father by his uncle Claudius. Hamlet, reclining with studied nonchalance in the foreground, ignores the action of the play, turning to study the gaze of steely, passionless cruelty with which King Claudius betrays his guilt. The Queen, Hamlet's mother, cowers in terror and shame as the truth of her first husband's murder is revealed, while the melancholy Ophelia sits with the vacant stare of latent madness. These effective portrayals convey a sense of the play's narrative and are indicative of Abbey's illustrator's eye. This, in addition to the beauty of the work with its jewel-like color and sumptuous textures, assured the popularity of the painting, which won three gold medals when it was later exhibited internationally.

Exhibitions: London: Royal Academy of Arts, 1897 (no. 477); Vienna: Vienna Jubilee Exhibition, 1898; Paris: Exposition Internationale, 1900; Berlin: International Exhibition, 1903; Liverpool: Dicksie & Co.,

1904; Irish-International Exhibition, 1903; British Exhibition, 1908; London: Royal Academy of Arts, 1912 (no. 469); New Haven: Yale University Gallery of Fine Arts, 1939 (no. 63); New York: American Academy of Arts and Letters, 1939 (no. 52); New Haven: Yale University Art Gallery, 1973 (no. 4) (traveling exhibition)

References:

The Academy, (May 8, 1897) p. 502

The Atheneum, (May 1, 1897) p. 582

Gazette des Beaux-Arts, (September, 1897) p. 256

Yale University Art Gallery, *Edwin Austin Abbey (1852-1911)* (New Haven: Yale University Art Gallery, 1974) p. 43, illus.

The Gallery/Stratford, *Fantastic Shakespeare* (Stratford, Ontario: The Gallery Stratford, 1978) fig. 14 illus.

---

1. See Martin Meisel, *Realizations*, (Princeton: Princeton University Press, 1983) especially chapter 3, "Speaking Pictures: the Drama," for a comprehensive discussion of the creative relationship between actors, artists and writers in the nineteenth century.

2. In E. V. Lucas, *The Life and Works of Edwin Austin Abbey*, R.A. (London and New York: Methuen, Scibner's, 1921 Vol I, p. 168), Abbey describes his conscientious approach to research: "My library has increased to a considerable extent...but even now I should feel justified in spending considerable sums upon works of reference." "I have laid out nearly £40 in books, costumes and architecture." p. 170.

3. Yale University Art Gallery, *Edwin Austin Abbey* (1852-1911), (New Haven: Yale University Art Gallery, 1974) p. 43.

2   See Plate I
Edwin Austin Abbey, N.A., R.A.
American, 1852-1911
The Penance of Eleanor, Duchess of Gloucester, 1900
Oil on canvas, 49 x 85
Signed and dated, lower left: E. A. Abbey, 1900
Museum of Art, The Carnegie Institute, Pittsburgh

In this picture, Abbey shows Eleanor Cobham, Duchess of Gloucester, who is accused of witchcraft and of conspiring against King Henry VI. As punishment she is sentenced to do public penance and banished to the Isle of Man. On her way to confinement she meets her husband, the Duke of Gloucester, and Abbey here represents her warning the Duke of his own impending fall.[1]

Abbey's large-scale paintings of Shakespearean subjects were inspired by a commission to illustrate the plays for *Harper's Monthly*. Characteristic of Abbey's work are the strict historical accuracy in the depiction of costume and faithful interpretation of Shakespeare's narrative. This painting was exhibited at the Carnegie Institute's Sixth Annual International Exhibition in 1901, and it was purchased for the Institute's own collection.

Exhibitions: London: The Royal Academy, 1900 (no. 147); Buffalo: The *Pan-American Exposition*, 1901; Pittsburgh: The Carnegie Institute, The Sixth Annual International Exhibition, 1901 (no. 1); Philadelphia: The Pennsylvania Academy of the Fine Arts (no. 25); Washington, D.C.: The Corcoran Gallery of Art, 1908; San Francisco: The California Palace of the Legion of Honor, *Panama-Pacific Exhibition*, 1915 (no. 2653); Dallas: Dallas Art Association, 1922; Washington: The Corcoran Gallery of Art, *The National Academy of Design Centennial Exhibition*, 1925 (no. 57); San Francisco: The California Palace of the Legion of Honor, 1926; New York: The American Academy of Arts and Letters, 1928; Newark: Newark Museum Association, 1930; Baltimore: The Baltimore Museum of Art, 1924; Richmond: The Virginia Museum of Fine Arts, 1936 (no. 79); Dayton: Dayton Art Institute, *American Expatriate Painters of the Late Nineteenth Century*, 1976-77 (traveling exhibition) (no. 2)

References:

Charles H. Caffin, *American Masters of Painting*, New York, 1902, pp. 91, 94, illus. opp. p. 86

E. V. Lucas, Edwin Austin Abbey, *Royal Academician, The Record of His Life and Work*, New York and London, 1921, vol. II, pp. 344, 346, 351, illus. opp. p. 352

Michael Quick, *American Expatriate Painters of the Nineteenth Century*, Dayton, Ohio: Dayton Art Institute, 1976, p. 82, illus. pl. I

---

1. There is an oil sketch in monochrome for this picture in the Edwin Austin Abbey Memorial Collection at the Yale University Art Gallery.

3
Edwin Austin Abbey, N.A., R.A.
American, 1852-1911
Goneril and Regan, 1902
Oil on canvas, 39¼ x 17½
Signed Lower left: E. A. Abbey/1902
The Edwin Austin Abbey Memorial Collection,
Yale University Art Gallery, New Haven, Connecticut

In publishing and theatrical circles Abbey was recognized as a preeminent interpreter of Shakespearean themes. *The Comedies of William Shakespeare* (a limited editon of 750 copies) was published in four volumes by *Harper's* in 1899, containing 131 illustrations. A companion publication illustrating the tragedies and histories was planned but never realized. The designs produced for this project were published individually in issues of *Harper's New Monthly Magazine* between 1902 and 1909. *Goneril and Regan* was one of four subjects from *Lear* published for an article on a play by Algernon Charles Swinburne in the December 1902 edition of *Harper's New Monthly Magazine.*[1]

The two models and their elaborate costumes relate to an earlier painting by Abbey, *King Lear,* Act I, scene i, 1898 (The Metropolitan Museum of Art). In that work, the two sisters dominate the left side of the canvas, forming part of a complex composition that depicts Lear's renunciation of Cordelia. The present work reverses the position of the figures, with Regan prominently placed in the foreground and the elder Goneril recessed in shadow. The similarity of costume and the Celtic motifs in the background suggest that Abbey produced this painting as a variation on the earlier image.[2] Although no specific incident is described, the figures' shifty-eyed and tight-lipped expressions suggest their later faithless betrayal of their father King Lear as they attempt to usurp his throne.

Exhibitions: London: Royal Academy of Arts, 1912 (no. 327); New York: American Academy of Arts and Letters, 1929 (no. 1); New Haven: Yale University Gallery of Fine Arts, 1939 (no. 66); New London, CT: Lyman Allyn Museum, 1945; Waterbury, CT: Mattatuck Historical Society, 1940; New Haven: Yale University Art Gallery, 1973 (no. 12) (traveling exhibition); Chadds Ford, PA: Brandywine River Museum, 1976; New York: Whitney Museum of American Art, 1977 (traveling exhibition)

References:

Harper's New Monthly Magazine, December 1902, frontispiece
Yale University Art Gallery, *Edwin Austin Abbey (1852-1911),* (New Haven: Yale University Art Gallery, 1974) p. 50, illus.
Patricia Hills, *Turn-of-the-Century America,* (New York: Whitney Museum of American Art, 1977) p. 99, fig. 115, illus.

1. Lucy Oakley points out that Abbey's illustrations for the comedies were reproduced in black and white, while this work was printed in color, a process not available to Abbey for large editions before the turn-of-the-century. He disliked the results of color printing, however, and returned to black and white.

2. Doreen Burke. *American Paintings in the Metropolitan Museum of Art.* vol. III (New York and Princeton: The Metropolitan Museum of Art and Princeton University Press, 1980) pp. 130-34. Abbey seems to have utilized the same costumes for both sets of figures. Regan wears a voluminous red dress with a broad pattern and Goneril a dark costume with cape. The artist may have adjusted the color (for example the lining of Goneril's cape) for compositional reasons. There is a throne behind the figure of Regan in the Metropolitan painting which features Celtic intertwined animal forms; and, although the throne is not repeated in the Yale painting, there is a band of repetitive design.

4   See Plate II
Washington Allston
American, 1779-1843
Falstaff Enlisting His Ragged Regiment at Justice Shallow's,
ca. 1806-08
Oil on canvas, 25¼ x 32½
Wadsworth Atheneum, Hartford, Gift from the existing Trustee of the Allston Trust

Among the earliest Shakespearean figures depicted in art was Sir John Falstaff, a popular and enduring character of both literature and legend.[1] His complex, yet immensely entertaining personality, made him a favored subject of many light-hearted scenes in the "low life" genre. Falstaff's character is developed over the course of three plays—the two parts of *Henry IV* and *The Merry Wives of Windsor*. The boon companion of young Prince Hal (later Henry V), Falstaff is central to the comic underplot which runs throughout the historical plays based on the reigns of the Lancasters. A rotund and jovial rascal, he is played off against the plays' noble characters, his good hearted clowning is contrasted with their harsher, more destructive pursuit of grandeur.

Here, Allston illustrates one of Falstaff's dubious schemes. In an episode from the second part of *Henry IV*, Falstaff enlists poor country yeomen into military service to replace wealthy landowners to whom he has previously sold discharges. His confederate Justice Shallow sits behind him, reading from a list of possible recruits and calling them forward to be questioned. Falstaff sneers and points in acceptance of the obsequious yokel before him as a dog sniffs suspiciously at the man's shoe. The work is an early effort by Allston, painted in Rome sometime between 1806 and 1808.[2]

A spirited and determined young man, Allston disappointed his genteel South Carolina family by insisting on a career as an artist. After his graduation from Harvard in 1800, he traveled to London and entered the Royal Academy as a pupil of Benjamin West. Sixteen months later he went to Paris with fellow artist and countryman John Vanderlyn, before moving on to Rome in 1805. There Allston developed the romantic landscape style for which he is best known. He also painted several Shakespearean subjects while in Italy, and returned to them periodically throughout his career.

His early interest in themes from Shakespeare may have been sparked by Fuseli's contributions to the Boydell Gallery which he could have seen as a young man in the engraved portfolio of that collection at the Charleston Library.[3] As a pupil of West's in London, Allston found much to admire in the literary subjects of the romantics such as John Opie, James Northcote and Fuseli himself, praising him for "his wild, romantic visions."[4] His friendship in Italy with the prominent poet and Shakespearean critic Samuel Taylor Coleridge nurtured his sensitivity to verse and may have encouraged these initial Shakespearean efforts.

The *Falstaff* . . . is painted in a style appropriate to its comic nature. It is set in a boxy, stage-like space reminiscent of a seventeenth-century Dutch interior. The broad treatment is derived from works by caricaturists such as Cruickshank, Gillray and Rowlandson, but Allston was also undoubtedly familiar with the version of the same subject by Hogarth.[5] He further experimented with this rather earthy style, which contrasts sharply with his poetic elegiac approach to landscapes and portraits, by painting a second farcical scene from Shakespeare, *Catherine and Petrucio, Grumio and the Tailor* (unlocated) in 1809.[6] A second episode from the life of Falstaff, in which he impersonates King Henry IV (*King Henry IV, Part I*, Act II, sc. iv) was composed on the grand scale of a history painting with lifesize figures. The present picture is probably the "little Falstaff" that Allston mentioned in a letter to John Vanderlyn, noting that he was taking it with him on his departure from Italy for America in 1808.[7]

References:
William H. Gerdts and Theodore E. Stebbins, Jr. *A Man of Genius: The Art of Washington Allston (1779-1843)* (Boston: The Museum of Fine Arts, 1979) p. 53, fig. 18
Edgar P. Richardson, *A Study of the Romantic Artist in America*, (Chicago: The University of Chicago, 1948) p. 188, no. 49

1. W. Moelwyn Merchant, *Shakespeare and the Artist* (London: Oxford University Press, 1959) p. 35.

2. Early accounts of the work give conflicting dates. See Edgar P. Richardson, *Washington Allston: A Study of the Romantic Artist in America* (Chicago: University Press, 1948) p. 193.

3. William Gerdts and Theodore Stebbins, Jr. *A Man of Genius: The Art of Washington Allston (1779-1843)* (Boston: Museum of Fine Arts, 1979) p. 25. The Boydell Gallery contained eight plates which included Falstaff: three each from *The Merry Wives of Windsor* and *Henry IV, Part I* and two from *Henry IV, Part II*. The plate which corresponds to Allston's subject, painted by J. Durno, engraved by T. Ryder, is set in a high ceilinged gothic hall, and Falstaff sits on a throne rather than at a table bearing no resemblance to the Allston. Other Boydell works, notably those however, by Smirke and Fuseli, may have suggested Falstaff's porcine face. The Boydell works had been issued collectively in 1803, about three years before Allston painted this work.

4. Richardson, p. 48.

5. Gerdts and Stebbins, p. 53-54. Hogarth's composition exists in several versions an early drawing of 1728 in the Royal Library at Windsor, a painting of 1730 also at Windsor and an engraving published May 1, 1799. Allston reverses Hogarth's composition, but adopts the pose of Falstaff and the recruit he questions, and the side lighting from an opposite window.

6. Allston adopted this atypical style for illustration of comic scenes from time to time. In addition to the two Shakespeare subjects he painted in 1811. *The Poor Author and the Rich Bookseller* (Boston Museum of Fine Arts). The rich bookseller is very similar in conception to Falstaff—seated at the left of the picture, extremely fat with a leering, pig-like face. See Richardson, p. 193 and Gerdts and Stebbins, p. 59.

7. C. R. Leslie wrote in letters of January 28, 1844 and September 6, 1844 to Richard Henry Dana regarding the "large Falstaff" which was supposedly shipped in cases of Allston's property, sent from Leghorn in 1816 or 17. See Richardson, p. 193 and Gerdts and Stebbins, p. 54.

5
Washington Allston
American, 1779-1843
The Opening of the Casket, ca. 1807
Oil on canvas, 19¾ x 24
The Boston Athenaeum, Boston, Massachusetts

Unlike the *Falstaff* . . . , Allston's *The Opening of the Casket* is suffused with the sense of poetic reverie most commonly associated with his work. Allston's approach is evident in the serenity and timelessness of this climatic moment in the second scene of the third act. Assembled are Portia, seated at the right with her attendants, with Bassanio, her chosen suitor, at the left. In order to win the beautiful heiress in marriage, Bassanio must choose from among three caskets the one that holds Portia's picture. With studied and graceful gesture, Bassanio indicates to Portia his choice—the leaden casket containing her image.

The graceful, almost sculptural stances of the figures and their balanced groupings reveal Allston's experiences within the schools of the French Academy, where he had studied prior to his Italian journey. There he was exposed to works by Jacques-Louis David and his pupils, and like them adopted the simplified shapes and compositional devices of Greek primitivism.[1] With his friend John Vanderlyn, Allston took delight in discovering the works of sixteenth-century Venetian masters, whose rich coloration, golden effects of light and sensuous evocation of an idealized past are evident in *The Opening of the Casket*.[2] Influenced by the Venetians, and the simplicity of Raphael's early work, this painting is believed to have been painted in Florence in 1807.[3]

Following his permanent return to the United States in 1818, Allston became extremely influential, respected as both an artist and scholar. He published a novel (*Monaldi*) inspired by his experiences of Italy and, posthumously, some poetry. He continued to utilize subjects from European literature, particularly Shakespeare. His later known works based on Shakespearean themes are known to include: *Hermia and Helena* from *A Midsummer Night's Dream* (exhibited R. A., 1818, now unlocated), an Italianate work from 1832 *Lorenzo and Jessica* from *The Merchant of Venice* (1832, Child's Gallery, Boston), and two unfinished works from the 1830s, *Death of King John* (1830s, Mugar Memorial Library, Boston University), and *Titania's Court* (1837, Vassar College, Poughkeepsie, NY).

Exhibitions: Bristol, England: Merchant Tailor's Hall, 1814; Brooklyn: Brooklyn Art Association, 1872 (no. 2); Boston: Boston Museum of Fine Arts, *Exhibition of the Works of Washington Allston*, 1881 (no. 206); Boston: Boston Museum of Fine Arts. *A Man of Genius: The Art of Washington Allston (1779-1843)*, 1979 (no. 18)

References:
William H. Gerdts and Theodore E. Stebbins, Jr. *A Man of Genius: The Art of Washington Allston (1779-1843)* (Boston: The Museum of Fine Arts, 1979) p. 53, no. 18 illus.
Edgar P. Richardson, *A Study of the Romantic Artist in America*. (Chicago: The University of Chicago, 1948) p. 192, no. 47
Diana J. Strazdes, "Washington Allston's Early Career, 1796-1811" (PhD Dissertation, Yale University, 1982) pp. 148-152
Moses F. Sweetser, *Allston*, (Boston, 1879) p. 187
Mabel Munson Swan, *The Athenaeum Gallery, 1827-1873* (Boston, 1940) p. 132
Jonathan P. Harding and Harry Katz, *The Boston Athenaeum Collection: Pre-Twentieth Century American and European Painting and Sculpture*, (Boston, 1984) pp. 12-13, illus. pl. 38

---

1. Dianna Strazdes, "Washington Allston's Early Career: 1796-1811" (PhD Dissertation, Yale University, 1982). Strazdes gives Raphael's Vatican fresco *Joseph Interpreting the Pharoah's Dream* as the source for this painting's composition. (See pages 148-152.)

2. William Gerdts and Theodore Stebbins, Jr. *A Man of Genius: The Art of Washington Allston (1779-1843)* (Boston: Museum of Fine Arts, 1979) p. 53.

3. According to the will of John E. Allston, who left the painting to the Boston Atheneum in 1877, the work was painted in Florence, 1807. Scholars have suggested other dates, see Gerdts and Stebbins, p. 53.

6
Henry Anelay
English, 1817-1883
Ferdinand and Miranda
Watercolor on paper, heightened with body colour, 23 x 17½
Signed at lower left: H. Anelay
Mr. and Mrs. E. Hal Dickson, Mr. and Mrs. James R. Duncan and Mr. and Mrs. Frank W. Rose, San Angelo, Texas

As they viewed this work by Henry Anelay, visitors to the Royal Watercolor Society's exhibition of 1852 would have appreciated its highly polished technique and satisfying moral message. Rather than illustrating a specific scene from the play, Anelay invents a visual conflation of three characters to represent the triumph of domestic happiness, one of the play's major themes and likewise an obsession of the Victorians.

The Tempest, which was first performed in celebration of a marriage during the winter of 1612 or 1613, has as its focus the reconciliation of art, nature and civilization, personified in the characters of Ferdinand and Miranda.[1] This mystical union is achieved by Prospero, Duke of Naples, a practitioner of white magic whose patient forbearance and learning conquer the forces of untamed nature. Anelay's Prospero, holding his book of magic, looks out from his cave to bless the betrothal of Ferdinand, the civilized prince, with his daughter Miranda, child of nature.

Anelay produced the setting for this ideal of marital harmony by following the Ruskinian dictum to paint nature truthfully, in all its detail. The closely observed flora, delicately tinted rock forms, even the small frog and bird (representing the creatures of land and air) symbolize Ruskin's Arcadian paradise where all conflict is banished. Ruskin's philosophy led the Pre-Raphaelites to paint similar direct translations of nature that attracted great public attention in the exhibitions of the early 1850s.

Anelay was primarily an illustrator for *The Illustrated London News* between 1843 and 1855, and contributed book illustrations for, among other volumes, *Merrie Days of England* and *Uncle Tom's Cabin*. While he exhibited occasionally at the Royal Academy, his works were more often seen at the Royal Society of British Artists in Suffolk Street.

Exhibition: London: The Royal Watercolor Society, 1852

---

1. The play was written to be performed as a part of the festivities surrounding the wedding of James I's daughter to Frederick, the Elector Palatine. Like Ferdinand and Miranda, they were scions of noble houses. The Victorians naturally drew parallels between these royal marriages and that of their own Queen, who wed Prince Albert of Saxe Coburg-Gotha in 1840.

7
Wolfgang Boehm
English (born Austria) active 1850-1869
A Scene from 'The Taming of the Shrew'
Oil on canvas, 49 x 69
Signed lower right: Böhm
Mr. and Mrs. E. Hal Dickson, Mr. and Mrs. James R. Duncan, and Mr. and Mrs. Frank W. Rose, San Angelo, Texas

The vogue for highly descriptive painting, that is literal visual translations of recognizable stories, was prevalent not only in England, but in northern Europe and America in the nineteenth century. Wolfgang Boehm, an English painter of Austrian origin, renders such an account of specific action from the fourth act of Shakespeare's *The Taming of the Shrew*.

In the process of "taming" his ill-tempered new bride, Petruchio pretends to find fault with a gown he has ordered for Katherine, pointing to indicate the offending sleeve he finds "carved like an apple tart." The Tailor, who has been given a written order by Petruchio's servant Grumio, scratches his head in perplexity as he reads the order. "Why here is the note of fashion to testify," he says.

Appropriately to the play's setting in Padua and Verona, Boehm has given the work a tripartite Italian High Renaissance style. On a shallow, boxy set the blind arches (one of which is an obvious backstage entrance) and the framing devices (such as the suggestion of a curtain on the left) communicate the theatrical intention. The tempestuous Katherine described by Shakespeare looks Flemish rather than Italian; Rubensian in proportion and complexion. The comic aspects of the scene are apparent in the gesture of the puzzled Tailor and the frustrated scowl and clenched fists of the "Shrew." The painter has obviously lavished his efforts upon the depiction of the various objects and sumptuous fabrics, chief among them being the disputed gown.

8
Philip Hermogenes Calderon, R.A.
English, 1833-1898
A Scene from 'Measure for Measure', 1873
Oil on canvas, 27¾ x 35¾
Signed and dated lower right: Calderon 1873
Mr. and Mrs. E. Hal Dickson, Mr. and Mrs. James R. Duncan and Mr. and Mrs. Frank W. Rose, San Angelo, Texas

Shakespeare's plays were used as sources for works of art in many different ways. Some painters reproduced specific actions, events characters in purely theatrical terms, while others composed imaginary situations based on their readings of the plays as literature. From a single quotation expressing "noble sentiment" for example, a painter might extrapolate an imaginary encounter of characters or visualize events left undescribed in the play itself.

Philip Hermogenes Calderon, a painter of history and genre scenes, presents just such a free interpretation of elements from the play *Measure for Measure*. In the play, Mariana is betrothed to Angelo, a deputy to the Duke of Vienna. When he learns that Mariana's brother has been lost at sea with her dowry, Angelo breaks the engagement. At the picture's exhibition at the Royal Academy in 1873, it was accompanied by a quotation from Act IV, scene i: "Take, O, take these lips away...," the lines sung by a boy to Mariana, alluding to this rejection. Calderon pictures Mariana recalling the moment at which Angelo disavows the engagement, although this episode actually occurs before the opening of the play and is not shown on stage. The discarded letter at the bottom left seems to indicate the receipt of bad news, prompting Angelo's withdrawal even as Mariana clings to him.

Mariana gained prominence in the Victorian period as a symbol of the rejected lover through the poem written by Alfred, Lord Tennyson of 1830. The Pre-Raphaelite John Everett Millais painted a *Mariana* in 1850-51 (The Makins Collection, London). Calderon, whose best-known work *Broken Vows* (1857, Tate Gallery, London) is painted in the Pre-Raphaelite style, has given the present painting a natural setting consistent with Pre-Raphaelite practice.

Calderon, the son of Juan Calderon, a Spanish priest who converted to the Protestant church and became a professor of literature at King's College, began his study of art in 1850 at the Leigh School in London and later journeyed to Paris, studying in the atelier of Francois Edouard Picot. A painter of genre, historical and religious subjects, Calderon enjoyed a successful career, elected an Associate of the Royal Academy in 1864, a full member in 1867, and Keeper of the Academy collection in 1887. He was the leader of the "St. John's Wood Clique," an informal group of artists who lived near one another in the London suburb of St. John's Wood during the 1860s and 70s and gathered together to sketch and for fellowship. Among the other members were John Evan Hodgson, G.D. Leslie and Henry Stacy Marks.

Exhibition: London: The Royal Academy, 1873 (no. 126)

9 See Plate III
Philip Hermogenes Calderon, R.A.
English, 1833-1898
The Young Lord Hamlet, 1868
Oil on canvas, 34½ x 55
Signed at lower right: Calderon
Mr. and Mrs. E. Hal Dickson, Mr. and Mrs. James R. Duncan and Mr. and Mrs. Frank W. Rose, San Angelo, Texas

In the Royal Academy Exhibition of 1868, Calderon exhibited another Shakespearean costume picture from *Hamlet* Act V, scene i. Calderon avoids the play's tragic themes by portraying the Prince of Denmark as a child before he grows into the melancholy young man of the play. The jester Yorick entertains the boy in a scene inspired by Hamlet's speech, "Alas poor Yorick...he hath borne me on his back a thousand times." The painting translates a Victorian family outing into a historical setting and is consistent with Calderon's preference for sentimental subjects. The viewer is left with a sense of foreboding only because of his knowledge of Yorick's and Hamlet's eventual fates.

Exhibition: London: The Royal Academy, 1868 (no. 316)

Reference:
W. Meynell, ed. *Some Modern Artists and Their Work*, London, 1883, p. 238

10
John Cawse
English, 1779-1862
Falstaff and Prince Hal
Oil on canvas, 27 × 32½
Mr. and Mrs. E. Hal Dickson, Mr. and Mrs. James R. Duncan and Mr. and Mrs. Frank W. Rose, San Angelo, Texas

John Cawse, trained as a political cartoonist, painted many versions of Sir John Falstaff and his adventures in a style that reflects his background in comic caricature.[1] As a portraitist and genre painter, Cawse exhibited at the Royal Academy, the British Institution in Suffolk Street, and the Old Water Colour Society between 1801 and 1845. In addition to Shakespearean scenes, he painted episodes from novels by Sir Walter Scott and Charles Dickens, as well as portraits of theatrical figures.[2]

Cawse here depicts one of the many verbal exchanges between Falstaff and the young Prince Hal. The old knight holds his sword and shield, relating the tale of his battle with "a hundred" thieves (who were in reality Hal himself and his companion Poins) in the first part of *Henry IV*, Act II, scene iv. Behind his back, Falstaff's band of rogues are laughing at his tall tale, with one thumbing his nose in contempt. The shallow space and light source from the left are standard elements in Cawse's depictions of Falstaff, and suggest the tradition of Hogarth, whose published engraving of Falstaff examining recruits (1799, The British Museum) is similarly constructed. The graceful figures of Prince Hal and Poins are consistent with the tradition of eighteenth-century book illustration derived from the style of French rococo and popularized in the Vauxhall Garden decorations of Francis Hayman in the 1740s and 50s.[3] Their elegant costumes resemble the traditional "masque" type used in the theatre during this period.

1. The Folger Shakespeare Library in Washington, D. C. has two Falstaff scenes by Cawse and a third is in the Yale Center for British Art, New Haven. One of the Folger scenes is a second version of Falstaff and Prince Hal; however, the composition is reversed with the Prince and Poins at the right. The other two works show Falstaff enlisting his recruits in Act three, scene two of *Henry IV Part II*. Cawse repeats many of the stock comic buffoon figures and bits of still life (such as armor) in each version.

2. Ulrich Thieme and Felix Becker. *Algemeines Lexikon Der Bildenden Kinstler.* vol. VI. Leizig: E. A. Seemann, 1912, p.238.

3. T. S. R. Boase, "Illustrations of Shakespeare's Plays in the Seventeenth and Eighteenth Centuries," *The Journal of the Warburg and Courtland Institutes*, vol. 10, (1947) pp. 89-90.

11 See Plate IV
Alexandre-Marie Colin
French, 1798-1875
The Three Witches from Macbeth, 1827
Oil on canvas, 29½ × 39½
Signed and dated at lower left: Colin Roma 1827
Mr. and Mrs. E. Hal Dickson, Mr. and Mrs. James R. Duncan and Mr. and Mrs. Frank W. Rose, San Angelo, Texas

As an aspect of Romanticism, the theory of the sublime (dread of the power of nature or other uncontrollable forces) was identified with Shakespearean subject matter in the eighteenth century by Henry Fuseli, William Blake and others who depended upon the so-called poetic imagination for inspiration. An accompanying fascination with the supernatural, and its embodiment in fantastic spiritual forms, existed well into the nineteenth century.

By the time Alexandre-Marie Colin painted *Macbeth*'s "three weird sisters," the image was popularly identified with the concept of human fate as revealed through prophetic power. Their depictions, both in the theatre and in art, were inevitably tied to the horrific apparitions they conjure for Macbeth in Act IV. From the early eighteenth century great care was lavished on elaborate effects on stage and in the illustrations to the printed plays representing the three malevolent hags pointing the way to Macbeth's destruction.[1]

Colin was one of a group of artists, which also included the Englishman Richard Parkes Bonington, surrounding the French Romantic painter Eugene Delacroix. Delacroix used as models for his own art works by a group of British artists that included Fuseli and his follower Robert Smirke, whose collection of forty Shakespearean subjects, published as *The Picturesque Beauties of Shakespeare*, Delacroix utilized between 1825 and 1850.[2] Like Delacroix, the artists in his circle chose subjects from English literature, such as the witches, that could be portrayed with less restraint than was customary in French academic art. Colin's composition follows that of several versions of this subject by Fuseli, but offers substantially more atmosphere.[3] The flash of lightning, the witches' grotesque faces, gnarled limbs and windswept hair are more unreservedly theatrical than Fuseli's classically sculptural figures, who glare in silent condemnation.

---

1. Esther Dotson, *Shakespeare Illustrated (1770-1820)*, PhD Dissertation, New York University, 1973, p. 158.

2. Esther Dotson, "English Shakespeare Illustration and Eugene Delacroix," *Essays in Honor of Walter Friedlaender (Marsyas, Supplement II)* New York: Institute of Fine Arts, New York University, 1965, p. 40.

3. Fuseli's painting is in the Royal Shakespeare Picture Gallery, Stratford-upon-Avon. The composition was reproduced in mezzotint in 1785 and engraved in 1786. See Geoffrey Ashton, *Shakespeare and British Art*, New Haven: Yale Center for British Art, 1981, p. 19.

12
George Cruickshank
English, 1792-1878
Pistol Informing Falstaff of the Death of Henry IV
Watercolor and pencil on paper, 4⅜ × 6⅞
Signed at lower right: George Cruickshank . . .
William A. Whitaker Collection
The Ackland Art Museum
Chapel Hill, North Carolina

The career of satirist and illustrator George Cruickshank spanned over fifty years of the nineteenth century, during which time he produced thousands of published designs. Although illustrations of Shakespearean subjects are not among Cruickshank's best-known work, he occasionally tried his hand at this popular source. As a friend of actor Edmund Kean, Cruickshank maintained an avid interest in "theatricals," and published several individual engravings of Kean in character (as Othello and Richard III, for example) and of groups from plays such as *Hamlet* and *Coriolanus*.[1]

Robert Brough's *Life of Sir John Falstaff*, published in 1858, was illustrated by Cruickshank with Shakespearean characters and scenes from plays featuring the old knight. *Pistol Informing Falstaff of the Death of Henry IV* corresponds generally to the plate on page 171, which represents *Henry IV, Part II*, Act V, scene iii.[2] In this scene the braggart soldier Pistol has come to Justice Shallow's garden to tell Falstaff that the young Prince Hal, Falstaff's former protege, has become King. While the fearful Justice remains glued to his seat with a look of apprehension, Falstaff stares in pop-eyed amazement at the implied good fortune.

Artists (Smirke for example) often endowed Falstaff with the decidedly unsavory aspect of a stock buffoon and scoundrel. Cruickshank, whose endlessly inventive satire is never malicious, envisions Falstaff as a puffed-up elf—gently innocuous and without sinister overtones. Cruickshank's thin, nervous line animates both the figures and their surroundings further emphasizing the excitement and anticipation inherent in the scene itself.

In his later years Cruickshank presented a number of paintings for the yearly exhibition in an attempt to establish his reputation as a serious artist. Among these were two Shakespearean subjects: *The Last Scene from the Merry Wives of Windsor* (1857, The Yale Center for British Art) and *The First Appearance of William Shakespeare on the Stage of the Globe with Part of His Dramatic Company in 1564* (1864-65, The Yale Center for British Art).

Exhibitions: Chapel Hill, NC: The William Hayes Ackland Memorial Art Center, *English Watercolors and Drawings 1700-1900*, 1975 (no. 19); Chapel Hill, NC: The William Hayes Ackland Art Center, *Six Centuries of Drawings in the Ackland Collection*, 1976

1. Cruickshank took part in many amateur productions, as did his friend and occasional collaborator Charles Dickens. On July 2, 1860, he appeared as Prospero in a burlesque production of *The Tempest* at Drury Lane. The performance was a benefit for the widow of Robert Brough, whose *Life of Falstaff* Cruickshank had just illustrated. William Feaver, *George Cruickshank* (London: Arts Council of Great Britain, 1974) pp. 5, 18. See also Albert Mayer Cohn, *George Cruickshank: A Catalogue Raisonné of the Work Executed During the Years 1806-1877*, catalogue numbers 1277 (Kean as Othello); 1278 (Kean as Richard III) 1177 (the characters of *Hamlet*) and 1018 (the characters of *Coriolanus*). Other Shakespearean subjects are nos. 108, 521, 693, 738, 871, 879, and 1901.

2. The watercolor may have been executed after the book design. In later years Cruickshank accepted commissions to reproduce his successful illustrations. See Catherine Johnson, *Catalogue of the Art Collection at the Folger Library* (unpublished) in her entry for Cruickshank and Feaver, p. 21.

13   See Plate X
Wladyslaw Von Czachorski
Polish, 1850-1911
The Actors Before Hamlet, 1875
Oil on canvas, 45¾ × 89
Mr. and Mrs. E. Hal Dickson, Mr. and Mrs. James R. Duncan and Mr. and Mrs. Frank W. Rose, San Angelo, Texas

With its frequent theatrical allusions clouding the distinction between reality and imagination, *Hamlet* is one of Shakespeare's most intensely psychological plays. The Polish artist Wladyslaw Von Czachorski visually suggests the delicate balance of passions which motivate the Prince as he seeks to avenge his murdered father.

When a group of traveling players arrives at Elsinore castle, Hamlet begins to formulate a plan which will reveal his uncle, now the King of Denmark, as his father's murderer. In an episode from Act II, scene ii, Hamlet, flanked by his friends Rosencrantz and Guildenstern on his right and the old courtier Polonius on his left, reveals his psychic torment through the tension in his body, which leans slightly away, and in his gesture, which seems designed to ward off the speech's effect on his disturbed mind. The courtiers' dark colored clothing contrasts with the bright red of the main actor's as he dramatizes the story requested by the Prince—one which recounts the slaughter of Priam from the tale of Dido and Aeneas. Hamlet's expression suggests that he is both intrigued and repelled by the revenge he plots.

The hyperrealism of this painting goes beyond the photographic in its detail. The viewer is enthralled by the palpable sense of place, and almost physically drawn into the intense emotional atmosphere which pervades the scene. The setting, costumes and arrangement of figures are as genuine as careful research into the play and historic sources can make them. (Note, for instance, the player in green at the right who is obviously a man dressed to resemble a woman.)

Czarchorski was a genre and portrait painter who studied at the Academies of Dresden and Munich. This painting won a gold medal at the Munich International Art exhibition when it was shown there in 1879.

Exhibitions: Munich: Kunstverein, 1875; Munich: International Kunstausstellung, 1879; Warsaw: Galerie Unger, 1879-80; Berlin: Kunstakademie, 1883; Lemberg: Ausstellung polnischer Kunst, 1894; Vienna: Kunstlerhaus, "Graflich, I. Milewski Sammlung" 1895; Vienna: C. Bednarczyk Gallery, "Bedeutende Gemlade polnischer Meister" 1969 (no. 58)

References:
A. Ryszkiewicz and J. Dabrowski, *Szekspir W Plastyce Polskiej* (Shakespeare and Polish Art), Breslau, 1965, pp. 30-34, pl. 14-19
B. Piatkowski, *Wladyslaw Czachorski*, Warsaw, 1927, pl. 5
C. Bednarczyk Gallery, *Bedeutende Gemalde polnischer Meister*, Vienna, 1969, no. 58, illus. cover
Sadakichi Hartmann, *Shakespeare in Art*, (Boston: L. C. Paget, 1900) pp. 284-287, illus. p. 285

14   See Plate V
Richard Dadd
English, 1819-1887
Titania Sleeping, ca. 1841
Oil on canvas, 25½ × 30½
Courtesy of Peter Nahum, London

Victorian interest in spiritualism and the occult encouraged the development of a unique painting genre involving the imaginary world of fairies. Two of Shakespeare's plays, *The Tempest* and *A Midsummer Night's Dream*, feature supernatural creatures which inspired many fairy painters, including Richard Dadd, one of the genre's outstanding practitioners.

In the present picture, the Fairy Queen's three attendants coax her into slumber with a lullaby while Oberon, barely visible in the cave behind her, waits to place a spell upon her when she sleeps.[1] Dadd ordered his composition in successive receding arches with a proscenium of bat wings and dwarf-like figures alluding to the stage associations.[2] The central characters, highlighted in the glow of reflected moonlight, are surrounded by minutely observed imps and flora, products of Dadd's exceptionally fertile imagination.

Dadd painted two other important Shakespearean works, *'Come unto these yellow sands'* (1842, Mr. and Mrs. John Rickett) from *The Tempest* and a second painting from *A Midsummer Night's Dream*, *Oberon and Titania* (1854/58, The Regis Collection, Minneapolis). He exhibited a *Puck* (private collection) at the Royal Academy in 1841 along with the *Titania Sleeping*. Dadd's creativity was apparently colored by his mental state—he suffered with depression for years before descending into total insanity in 1843. He continued to paint after being committed to an insane asylum and produced his best-known work, *The Fairy Teller's Master Stroke* (1855-64, Tate Gallery) during his confinement.

Exhibitions: London: The Royal Academy, 1841 (no. 207); Manchester: *Art Treasurers of the United Kingdom*, 1857 (no. 477); London: The Tate Gallery, *The Late Richard Dadd*, 1974-75 (no. 57)

References:
David Greysmith, *Richard Dadd; the rock and castle of seclusion*, London: Studio Vista, 1873, pp. 75-76, 170, illus. pl. 25
Patricia Allderidge, *The Late Richard Dadd*, London: The Tate Gallery, 1974, pp. 59, 61, illus. p. 60

---

1. The painting was exhibited with a quotation from Act II, scene i: "There sleeps Titania sometimes of the night lulled in these flowers with dances and delight."

2. Patricia Allderidge, *The Late Richard Dadd*, London: The Tate Gallery, 1974, p. 61. Allderidge proposes several compositional sources for the work including Daniel Maclise's *Choice of Hercules*, (ca. 1831, collection of the Hon. C. Lennox-Boyd), Georgione's *Adoration of the Shepherds* (National Gallery, Washington, D.C.) and Fuseli's *Vision of the Madhouse* (Kunsthaus, Zurich).

15
Nathaniel Dance-Holland, R. A.
English, 1736-1811
David Garrick as Richard III
Oil on canvas, 37½ × 23¼
Mr. and Mrs. E. Hal Dickson, Mr. and Mrs. James R. Duncan and Mr. and Mrs. Frank W. Rose, San Angelo, Texas

Some of the best-known of all Shakespearean theatrical portraits are those of the actor and impresario David Garrick in his premier role as Richard III. Nathaniel Dance's painting, exhibited at the Royal Academy exhibition of 1771, was one of dozens of portraits of Garrick which were frequently reproduced for the theatre-going public of the eighteenth century. The original work, which measures seven by four feet and now hangs in the town hall at Stratford-on-Avon, was commissioned by Garrick himself.[1] This painting is one of many extant smaller versions, and may have been painted for a member of Garrick's family.[2]

Dance belonged to the fashionable literary and artistic world which surrounded Garrick, and documented his theatrical revolution. As the eighteenth century's most famous actor, Garrick is credited with introducing a natural style which incorporated elements of intellectual interpretation and psychological subtlety, and with the use of period costume to enhance historical accuracy. Garrick produced twenty-four of Shakespeare's plays when he was the manager of the Drury Lane Theatre, and, in 1769, organized the Shakespeare Jubilee at Stratford. His enthusiasm and promotion of Shakespeare's work greatly stimulated the public's interest in the plays and contributed to their use as subjects for engravings and paintings. He was closely associated with the role of Richard III, which he first acted in 1741 at the Goodman's Fields Theatre. Dance depicts the battle of Bosworth Field as a backdrop for the actor, who lunges forward exhorting his troops in what will be the fatal confrontation with Henry Tudor. This smaller work faithfully reproduces the larger canvas, which was clearly intended to represent the intensity of Garrick's stage performance in the dramatic expression of his face and clenched fist.

The son of architect George Dance, Nathaniel studied under Francis Hayman (1708-1776) a history painter and illustrator of Shakespearean scenes. Dance retired on his inheritance in 1776, later married a rich widow and was made a baronet, taking on the name Dance-Holland.

1. Garrick was painted at least three times in the role of Richard III—by William Hogarth in 1746, by Francis Hayman in 1760 and by Dance in 1771. Hogarth's painting (fig. 1, Oakley essay) depicts the tent scene. Hayman's and Dance's are very similar standing portraits, down to the use of sword and clenched fist. As a pupil of Hayman's, Dance probably knew the earlier battle scene. Garrick was regularly painted both in character and out, by the many artists of his acquaintance including Joshua Reynolds, Henry Fuseli and Johann Zoffany.

2. The work was engraved by Dixon and published by John Boydell in 1772. The National Theatre Collection in London has a copy believed to have been made after the mezzotint engraving by Dixon. See Raymond Mander and Joe Mitcheson, *The Artist and the Theatre*. (London: William Heinemann, Ltd, 1955) p. 181. The Folger Library in Washington also has a copy of the work which was acquired in 1925 from Curtis Walters.

16
Charles Edouard Delort
French, 1841-1895
Romeo and Juliet—Capulet's Garden
Oil on panel, 22 x 16
Signed, lower left: C. DELORT
Mr. and Mrs. E. Hal Dickson, Mr. and Mrs. James R. Duncan and Mr. and Mrs. Frank W. Rose, San Angelo, Texas

The French painter Charles Delort has chosen to represent one of the best-known of all scenes from Shakespeare—the encounter of Romeo and Juliet in the Capulet's garden. The artist's emphasis is clearly on the setting—the passageway, surmounted by a pierced Gothic-revival pediment and shrouded in mysterious shadow, predominates over the figures. Although Shakespeare's balcony scene takes place at night, Delort's representation is flooded with the bright sun of midday. The artist also furnishes Romeo with a lute, a traditional instrument of courtship. Such departures from and embellishments of the text are typical of the license many nineteenth-century artists took with Shakespeare's popular subjects.

Delort was a pupil of Jean León Gerôme. He exhibited many literary subjects at the French Salon, beginning in 1866 with a *Daphnis and Chloe*.

17 See Plate VI
Walter Howell Deverell
English, (Born America) 1827-1854
Twelfth Night, 1850
Oil on canvas, 52¼ x 40
The FORBES Magazine Collection, New York

Walter Howell Deverell was never an official member of the Pre-Raphaelite Brotherhood, but was closely associated with the group through his friendship with Dante Gabriel Rossetti. The two had met as students at Sass's drawing school in 1843 and at the Royal Academy Antique School in 1846.[1] Thematically, this scene from Shakespeare's *Twelfth Night* is consistent with the romances from classical Italian and medieval sources which Rossetti proposed as appropriate pictorial subjects for members of the Brotherhood.

The central figure, Orsino, listens with a distracted and pensive expression as the Clown sings of death and unrequited love. To his right is Viola, disguised as a boy, gazing fondly at the Duke, whom she loves despite his infatuation with another. Like many of the Pre-Raphaelites, Deverell used members of the circle as models for the figures in the painting, even portraying himself as the love-sick Orsino. He persuaded a beautiful shopgirl, Elizabeth Siddal, to sit for Viola.[2] Thus introduced, Siddal became one of the most important of the Pre-Raphaelites' female icons and later the wife of Rossetti, who appears as the Clown, Feste, to the Duke's left. The brilliant, light-filled composition ignores academic conventions: the relationship among the various architectural elements is ambiguous and the sunlight seems to stream from inside the building to cast long, mysterious shadows.

The Pre-Raphaelite Brotherhood, founded by William Holman Hunt, Dante Gabriel Rossetti, and John Everett Millais in 1848, was a short-lived but influential society of painters who rejected the academic tenets of the prevailing artistic establishment in an attempt to rediscover the fervour and "moral seriousness" of earlier painting. Inspired by the art critic John Ruskin, who later became their apologist, the young painters overcame the public's initial hostility and found a wide audience for their works. Deverell held great promise as one of the Pre-Raphaelites' most talented followers but, tragically, died at the age of twenty-seven leaving this painting as his major work.

Exhibitions: London: National Institute, 1850; Birmingham, England: City of Birmingham Art Gallery, *Pre-Raphaelite Brotherhood 1848-1862*, 1947 (no. 22); London: The Tate Gallery (loan 1966-1972); Baden-Baden: Staatliche Kunsthalle, *Praraffaeliten*, 1973-74 (no. 87); Philadelphia Museum of Art, 1979; London: The Tate Gallery, *The Pre-Raphaelites*, 1984 (no. 23); Tokyo: *The Pre-Raphaelites and Their Times*, 1985 (no. 8)

References:
William Michael Rossetti, "Some Portraits of D. G. Rossetti," *The Magazine of Art*, 1885, p. 26
Esther Wood, *Dante Rossetti*, London: 1893, pp. 99-100
Percy H. Bate, *The English Pre-Raphaelite Painters*, London, 1899, pp. 43-54, illus. p. 54
H. C. Marillier, *Dante Gabriel Rossetti*, London, 1901, p. 17
William Holman Hunt, *Pre-Raphaelitism and the Pre-Raphaelite Brotherhood*, Oxford, 1905, pp. 197-99
Bryan's Dictionary of Painters and Engravers, II, London, 1919, illus. p. 64
Sadakichi Hartmann, *Shakespeare in Art*, Boston, 1901, pp. 165-66
William Gaunt, *The Pre-Raphaelite Dream*, Oxford, 1943, pp. 44-45
John Gere and Reubin Ironside, *Pre-Raphaelite Painters*, London, 1948, p. 48
Oswald Doughty, *A Victorian Romantic*, London, 1960, pp. 117-18
G. H. Flemming, *Rossetti and the Pre-Raphaelite Brotherhood*, London, 1967, pp. 128-136
John Nicol, *The Pre-Raphaelites*, London, 1969, p. 57, illus. no. 41
William Guant, *The Restless Century: Painting in Britain 1800-1900*, London, 1972, illus. pl. 81
Staatliche Kunsthalle Baden-Baden, *Praraffaeliten*, Baden-Baden, 1973, illus. p. 158
Timothy Hilton, *The Pre-Raphaelites*, London, 1974, pp. 51-52, illus. p. 53
William Fredman, *The P.R.B. Journal*, Oxford, 1975, p. xx
James Hardin, *The Pre-Raphaelites*, London, 1977, p. 42
Christopher Wood, *The Pre-Raphaelites*, London, 1977, p. 42
Christopher Wood, *The Pre-Raphaelites*, New York, 1981, pp. 15-16, illus. p. 16
The Tate Gallery, *The Pre-Raphaelites*, London, 1984, p. 74, illus. p. 74

---

1. William Gaunt, *The Restless Century: Painting in Britain 1800-1900*, London: Phaidon Press, Ltd., p. 106.

2. Dante Gabriel Rossetti assisted Deverell in painting the head of Siddal as Viola. See The Tate Gallery, *The Pre-Raphaelites*, London: The Tate Gallery/Penguin Books, 1984, p. 73. Siddal posed for two other important Pre-Raphaelite paintings with Shakespearean themes: John Everett Millais' *Ophelia* (1851-52 Tate Gallery) and William Holman Hunt's *Valentine Rescuing Sylvia from Proteus* (1850-51, Birmingham City Museum and Art Gallery). Christopher Wood, *The Pre-Raphaelites*, New York: Viking Press, 1981, p. 27.

18
Samuel De Wilde
English, 1748-1832
Robert Coates as Romeo, ca. 1812
Pencil and watercolor on paper, 13 x 8¼
Inscribed, lower left: [illegible]
The Garrick Club, London

Samuel De Wilde was a well-known theatrical portraitist in late eighteenth-century London. At his studio located between Covent Garden and Drury Lane he recorded the appearances of the era's most famous actors in a long series of portraits, later given wide distribution in the serial publications of the day. His illustrations for John Cawthorn's *Minor British Theatre*, William Oxberry's *New English Drama*, John Bell's *British Theatre*, and other periodicals, are among the most enduring accomplishments of his career.

The subject of this painting is the actor Robert Coates, nicknamed Romeo Coates because of his association with the role.[1] Born to a wealthy colonial family on the island of Antigua, Coates later settled in Bath, where he displayed a magnificent collection of diamonds along with some talent as an actor. After moderate success in the theatre, Coates went bankrupt, and retired to Boulogne to escape his creditors. He eventually returned to England, and died in February 1848 after being crushed between a hansom cab and a private carriage following his attendance at a performance at Drury Lane.

De Wilde was one of the first students accepted into the Royal Academy Schools in 1769. His exhibition career began with a 1776 exhibition at the Society of Artists and spanned half a century. With the exception of a few satirical scenes, De Wilde primarily painted watercolors in the manner of *Robert Coates as Romeo*. The format of single figures in costume was dictated by the theatrical publications and by the individual commissions he received from the actors and their admirers.[2] Contemporaries praised De Wilde for the accuracy of his portraits' likenesses and they are an outstanding source of information on costuming of the day.[3]

Exhibition: London: Guildhall Art Gallery, *Shakespeare and the Artist*, 1964 (no. 29)

References:
C. K. Adams, A Catalogue of the Pictures in the Garrick Club, London: Garrick Club, 1935, no. 523.
John Genest, *Some Accounts of the English Stage from the Restoration in 1660 to 1830* Vol. VIII (Bath: H. C. Carrington, 1832) p. 207
Charles Mathews, *Catalogue of Charles Mathews Collection*, London, 1833, cat. no. 250
Guildhall Art Gallery, *Shakespeare and the Theatre*, London: Guildhall Art Gallery, 1964, p. 17

1. The work was engraved in 1812; see *Catalogue of Dramatic Portraits in the Theater Collection of the Harvard College Library* (Cambridge, Mass: Harvard University Press, 1930-34) vol. I, s.v. "Coates, Robert," no. 4

2. A number of De Wilde's paintings survive in dramatic collections such as that of the National Theatre, which owns forty-three. See Geoffrey Ashton, "The Somerset Maugham Theatre Collection," *The Connoisseur* 120 (1981) 142-46.

3. Northampton Museums and Art Gallery, *Samuel De Wilde/George James De Wilde* (Northampton: Museums and Art Gallery, 1971) p. 8.

19
Thomas Francis Dicksee
English, 1819-1895
Ophelia, 1864
Oil on academy board, 16½ x 11½
Inscribed with monogram and dated lower right: 18/TFD/64
On verso: labeled: #21 Ophelia/Good my lord, how does your honour for this many a day? (*Hamlet*, Act 3, scene i)
T. F. Dicksee
7 Rudsell Place, Fitzroy Square
Mr. and Mrs. E. Hal Dickson, Mr. and Mrs. James R. Duncan and Mr. and Mrs. Frank W. Rose, San Angelo, Texas

Shakespeare's heroines won wide popularity in the nineteenth century as the personifications of feminine virtue. From the noble, intelligent Portia to the chaste Miranda, the major female characters were codified as role models for Victorian girls by writers such as Mary Cowden Clarke and Anna Jameson.[1]

Of all these female characters, Victorians attached the strongest sentiment to Ophelia, a pathetic and innocent figure who is brought to destruction through irresistible forces outside her control. Dicksee represents the aftermath of her encounter with Hamlet in Act III, scene i, wherein he viciously denies his previous affection for her and denounces all women. Ophelia's wounded look of despair and betrayal as she clutches her body protectively foreshadows her loss of reason.

Thomas Francis Dicksee was a portrait and figure painter who began his career at the age of nineteen as a student of Henry Perronet Briggs (?1791-1844), an artist best known for his own Shakespearean subjects.[2] Dicksee became associated with the depiction of Shakespearean heroines, exhibiting seven at the Royal Academy and contributing five to Mary Cowden Clarke's *Girlhood of Shakespeare's Heroines*.[3] He was the father and teacher of three prominent artists: Sir Frank Dicksee, Margaret Isabel Dicksee and Herbert Thomas Dicksee.

1. Nineteenth-century portraits of Shakespearean heroines were the subject of an exhibition, *Shakespeare's Heroines in the Nineteenth Century*. Buxton Museum and Art Gallery, 1980, Geoffrey Ashton.

2. Jeremy Maas, *Victorian Painters* (New York: G. P. Putnam's Sons, 1969) p. 110.

3. *Shakespeare's Heroines in the Nineteenth Century*, p. 12.

20
Augustus Leopold Egg
English, 1816-1863
Scene from The Taming of the Shrew, 1860
Oil on canvas, 16 x 27
Signed and dated lower left: Aug Egg 1860
Mr. and Mrs. E. Hal Dickson, Mr. and Mrs. James R. Duncan, and Mr. and Mrs. Frank W. Rose, San Angelo, Texas

After study at Sass's Art School and at the Royal Academy Schools, Egg expressed his dissatisfaction with Academy strictures and precepts by joining The Clique.[1] Among his other Shakespearean subjects were *Launce's Substitute for Proteus' Dog* (1849, Leicester Museums and Art Gallery), commissioned for Isambard Kingdom Brunel's Shakespeare Room, and his contributions to Charles Heath's gallery of Shakespearean heroines, published in 1836-37.

Augustus Leopold Egg is today remembered for his striking triptych of contemporary Victorian life, *Past and Present* (1858, Tate Gallery), but the majority of his works represent scenes from history and literature. A gifted actor, Egg performed regularly with Charles Dickens' amateur company; his paintings of subjects from dramatic literature show an actor's appreciation for characterization and narrative.

In the *Taming of the Shrew*, Act IV, sc. i, Petruchio teaches his hungry and disagreeable new wife Katherine a lesson in obedience by denying her the leg of mutton, which he declares to be "burnt." Egg has arranged Petruchio, Katherine and the servants in a shallow, stage-like space. The draped background, with its paired entrances, focuses interest on the boisterous events in the foreground as a glowering Petruchio pulls the tableware to the floor, waving a knife in one hand and the mutton in the other. The work is one of at least four paintings by Egg with subjects drawn from *The Taming of the Shrew*, and may have been his final composition before his death in 1863. Like many of Egg's late paintings, the work reveals his admiration of the precise draughtsmanship and striking coloration of the Pre-Raphaelites.[2]

Exhibitions: London: The Royal Academy, 1860 (no. 275); Manchester: *The Royal Jubilee Exhibition*, 1887 (no. 713); London: The Arts Council of Great Britain, *Shakespeare in Art*, 1964 (no. 52); London: Roy Miles, *Important Victorian Paintings*, 1976.

References:

The Arts Council of Great Britain, *Shakespeare in Art*. Essay by William Moelwyn Merchant, Catalogue by Ronald Pickvance, London: The Arts Council, 1964, p. 25

Hilarie Faberman. *Augustus Leopold Egg, R.A. (1816-1863)*, PhD Dissertation, Yale University, 1983, pp. 300-302; 80, illus. 80a

1. The Clique was composed of Richard Dadd, John Phillip, H. N. O'Neil, W. P. Frith and Egg. They were an important precursor of the Pre-Raphaelite Brotherhood in their attitude towards the Royal Academy, but their aesthetic aims were widely divergent and they never coalesced into a coherent movement.

2. Hilarie Faberman, *Augustus Leopold Egg, R.A. (1816-1863)*, PhD Dissertation, Yale University, 1983, pp. 300-303, p. 502. Faberman notes that there are two versions of this composition, the larger of which is presently unlocated. It is unclear which of the two versions was shown at the Royal Academy in 1860 (see Faberman, p. 503). The provenances are also confused; one of the two versions was commissioned by Thomas Agnew. Faberman lists two other compositions for *The Taming of the Shrew* (unlocated) which may relate to the present work or to other scenes by Egg from this play (see nos. 49 and 50).

21 See Plate VII
Alfred W. Elmore, R.A.
English (born Ireland), 1815-1881
Much Ado About Nothing, 1846
Oil on canvas, 40 x 78
Signed and dated at lower left: A Elmore 1846
Mr. and Mrs. E. Hal Dickson, Mr. and Mrs.
James R. Duncan and Mr. and Mrs. Frank W.
Rose, San Angelo, Texas

In *Much Ado About Nothing,* Elmore represented the most dramatic, and the only serious episode, from one of Shakespeare's most joyous and lighthearted comedies. This pivotal scene is charged with the seriousness and emotional intensity that Victorian audiences expected to find in important history pictures.

In this scene Claudio falsely accuses Hero of infidelity and refuses to marry her. Shocked by the accusation, Hero sinks into unconsciousness as Claudio is hurried away from the altar by his scheming companion Don John, the instigator of the mischief. While the attention of the attendants is directed toward the swooning Hero, her father Leonato stares out of the canvas, his hand held to his head in disbelief at the turn of events. The remainder of the play is spent resolving this crisis.

Elmore was a respected member of the Royal Academy and enjoyed a successful, if not stellar, career. A reviewer for the *Athenaeum* magazine said that Elmore's paintings were those "such as engraver's revel in the public purchase. There is nothing to dazzle and astonish, but everything to calmly delight."[1] Elmore's subjects derived from historic or literary sources were popular; their stylistic debt to Italian Renaissance art is apparent. Hero and her attendants are the sensual and voluptuous Italian women derived from the works of Michaelangelo or Titian. Elmore combines these influences with a Victorian's sensitivity to the details of costume and setting to produce this accomplished result.

Initially learning to draw from sculptures in the British Museum, Elmore entered the Royal Academy Schools in 1833, and spent the formative years of his art training travelling the Continent studying in Paris, Munich and eventually Rome. He exhibited at the Royal Academy between 1834 and 1880. He was elected an associate of the Royal Academy in 1845 and Academician in 1857. Among his other Shakespearean subjects were *Lady Macbeth* (1849), *Hotspur and the Fop* (1851), *Katherine and Petruchio* (1869), a scene from "The Merchant of Venice" (Act II, sc. vii) and a *Romeo and Juliet,* now in the collection of the Walker Art Gallery, Liverpool.[2]

Exhibitions: London: The Royal Academy, 1846 (no. 471)

---

1. As quoted in Jeannie Chapel, *Victorian Taste,* (London: A Zwemmer, Ltd., 1982) p. 81.

2. Geoffrey Ashton, *Shakespeare's Heroines in the Nineteenth Century* (Buxton: Museum and Art Gallery, 1980) p. 16, note 4.

**22
Alfred W. Elmore,** R.A
English (born Ireland), 1815-1881
Two Gentlemen of Verona, 1857
Oil on canvas, 27 x 20½
Signed and dated at lower left: A. Elmore 1857
Royal Academy of Arts, London

Elmore exhibited this painting in 1858 with a quotation from Act III: "This love of theirs myself have often seen,/ Haply when they have judged me fast asleep." The reference is to the lovers in the play, Sylvia and Valentine, who are secretly observed by the Duke of Milan, who is seated in the foreground of the painting.

Like Elmore's *Much Ado About Nothing,* this is a costume piece strongly influenced by the art of the Italian Renaissance. A notebook from the period of Elmore's residence in Italy contains what may be a study for the Duke as he is depicted here.[1]

Exhibitions: London: The Royal Academy, 1858 (no. 120). Buxton: Buxton Museum and Art Gallery, *Shakespeare's Heroines in the Nineteenth Century,* 1980 (no. 6)

Reference:

Geoffrey Ashton. *Shakespeare's Heroines in the Nineteenth Century,* Buxton: Buxton Museum and Art Gallery, 1980, p. 16, illus.

---

1. See Geoffrey Ashton, *Shakespeare's Heroines in the Nineteenth Century* (Buxton: Buxton Museum and Art Gallery, 1980) p. 16, illus.

23 See Plate VIII
John Faed, R.S.A
Scottish, 1820-1902
Shakespeare and His Contemporaries
Oil on canvas, 53 x 68
Mr. and Mrs. E. Hal Dickson, Mr. and Mrs. James R. Duncan and Mr. and Mrs. Frank W. Rose, San Angelo, Texas

Shakespeare's reputation as a giant in English history and literature assured his status as a cult figure in the nineteenth century. This painting by John Faed presents Shakespeare as "first among equals" in a gathering of the most prominent literary figures of his era.[1]

Also known as *Shakespeare and His Friends at the Mermaid Tavern*, the work became widely known and admired through contemporary engravings.[2] It probably represents the artist's imaginary reconstruction of a Friday Street Club meeting at the Mermaid. The Club was founded by Sir Walter Raleigh (here pictured in red hose and gold doublet, leaning against the chimneypiece), and its members were the outstanding intellectuals of London at the time. The Mermaid was located in Broad Street to the east of St. Paul's, with an entrance bordering Friday Street. There is no evidence that Shakespeare frequented the Club, but his close friend and trustee of his will, William Johnson, was the Mermaid's proprietor. Faed carefully organized the groups of figures to focus on the centrally placed Shakespeare. The composition suggests he was inspired by the many seventeenth-century Dutch group portraits of merchants and businessmen by artists such as Rembrandt and Franz Hals in which the figures are arranged along a horizontal plane, related to one another through pose and glance. Faed painted a similar piece titled *Sir Walter Scott and His Literary Friends at Abbotsford*.

John Faed was a member of a Scottish family of artists which included his brothers James, Thomas and George. He began his career between the ages of eleven and twelve as a miniaturist, traveling to the villages near his home at Gatehouse to execute portraits of the aristocracy. He studied at the Art School of the Trustees of the Board of Manufacturer's, becoming proficient enough as a history and genre painter to secure his election to the Royal Scottish Academy in 1851. In 1864 he moved to London where he exhibited regularly at the Royal Academy.[3]

Exhibitions: Washington, D.C.: Folger Shakespeare Library, 1933-34; Washington, D.C.: George Washington University, 1952

References:

Art Journal, October 1871, pp. 237-239
  Sadakichi Hartman, *Shakespeare in Art,* Boston: L.C. Paget, 1900, p. 25, illus. following p. 22
Virginia LaMar, "William Shakespeare" *Collier's Merit, Student's Encyclopedia* vol XVI, p. 574. illus.

1. Those portrayed are, from the left, William Camden (1551-1623); Thomas Sackville, Earl of Dorset (1536-1608); John Selden (1584-1654); Francis Beaumont (1584-1616); John Fletcher (1579-1625); Francis Bacon (1561-1626); Ben Johnson (1572-1637); Samuel Daniel (1562-1619); John Donne (1573(?)-1631); Walter Raleigh (152(?)-1618); Henry Wriothesley, Earl of Southhampton (1573-1624); Robert Cotton (1571-1631) and Thomas Dekker (1570-1632(?)). The figures are identified on the mezzotint engraved by John Faed's brother James.

2. James Faed's engraving of his brother's composition which was published by James Keigh 60 Prince's Street, Edinburgh. A second engraving was made by John Sartain of Philadelphia in two versions, one of which identifies the sitters, the other which does not. See the Folger catalogue of art S52F.4 no. 5 26 b copy 1 & 2 and 26 d-e. A second larger version (25 x 30½") is undated. See the Folger art catalogue S527F.4 no 26a.

3. The work of the Faed family is the subject of Mary McKerrow, *The Faeds,* (Edinburgh: Cannongate Publishing, Ltd., 1982).

24   See Plate IX
Henry Fuseli, , R.A.
English, (born Switzerland) 1741-1825
Lady Constance, Arthur, Salisbury, 1783
Oil on paper, 25 x 21
Smith College Museum of Art, Northampton, Massachusetts, Purchased with the Gift of Eleanor Lamont Cunningham

The intensity of Shakespeare's great tragic themes—jealousy, despair, destruction—was realized in the work of his most prolific and influential interpreter, Henry Fuseli. The strong emotional character of Fuseli's *Lady Constance, Arthur, Salisbury* is indicative of his belief that Shakespeare was "the great instructor of Mankind" in his ability to demonstrate the bitter nature of uncontrolled human passion.

The subject of Lady Constance mourning, which Fuseli repeated several times between 1783 and 1825[1] is taken from Act III, scene i of Shakespeare's *King John.* Her son, Arthur, a claimant to the English throne, reclines listlessly in the foreground, his hopes for succession crushed by the defection of his French and Austrian allies. His sense of melancholy distraction is echoed in the background by the figure of Salisbury, who has delivered the news of the desertion.

The painting's three figures are powerfully conceived, their physically massive bodies and poses derived from classical prototypes.[2] The serenity and stability associated with such compositions is missing in this work, however, replaced by a sense of dread and irrational terror. Fuseli's is a richly symbolic art in which Constance, with her violently clenched fists and ravaged face, goes beyond a depiction of maternal grief to embody the larger sense of tragic loss central to Shakespeare's play.

An eighteenth-century scholar of the Germanic *Sturm und Drang* tradition, Fuseli was fascinated with Shakespeare. He had translated *Macbeth* into German and executed many drawings from *Lear* and *Macbeth* before he journeyed to London in 1864. From 1770 to 1778 he lived in Italy, occupied with study of Michaelangelo and theories of the sublime. On his return to England he developed a circle of literary and theatrical friends (his sketchbooks indicate his frequent attendance at Garrick's Shakespeare performances), who influenced his choice of subjects and supported his philosophical theories of art.[3] He was a key contributor to the Boydell Shakespeare Gallery project (he developed a similar Milton Gallery of his own), and illustrated a major edition of the plays, published by F. C. and J. Rivington in 1805. He ended his career as Professor of Painting at the Royal Academy, giving lectures there in 1801 and 1805 which summarized his system of painting, establishing its wide-ranging influence on contemporaries and younger artists.

Exhibitions: London: The Royal Academy, 1783 (no. 209); New York: Durlacher Brothers, *Romanticism in Eighteenth Century England,* 1953 (no. 9); Fitchburg, Massachusetts: *18th Century Portraits and Landscapes by Famous Painters of the British School,* 1955 (no. 11); Cambridge, Massachusetts: Fogg Art Museum, Harvard University, *Sublimity and Sensibility: The Genesis of Romanticism,* 1965 (no. 9); Zurich, Switzerland: Kunsthaus Zurich, *Johann Heinrich Fussli,* 1969 (no. 9); Hamburg, West Germany: Kunsthalle, *Henry Fuseli 1741-1825,* (traveling exhibition) 1975 (no. 64); Stratford, Ontario: The Gallery/Stratford, *Fantastic Shakespeare,* 1978 (no. 24)

References:
Smith College Museum of Art, *Bulletin,* nos. 29-32, June 1951, p. 22
Henry A. Lafarge, "Fuseli and Early Romantics," *Art News,* January, 1953 pp. 32, 60 illus.
Peter Tomory, *The Life and Art of Henry Fuseli,* New York: Praeger, 1972, pp. 95-96 illus.
Gert Schiff, *Johann Heinrich Fussli, 1741-1825,* Zurich: Schweizerisches Institute for Kunstwissenshaft, 1973, no. 722, vol. I, p. 490 (illus.) vol. II, p. 169

---

1. The iconography of Lady Constance mourning and its several versions are discussed in Esther Gordon Dotson, *Shakespeare Illustrated 1780-1820* (PhD Dissertation, New York University, 1973) pp. 419-424.

2. The crouching figure of Constance is derived from one of the Ancestor figures of the Sistine Ceiling, the *Jesse* spandrel. Dotson, p. 421. Similarly, the figure of Arthur is an adaption of the poses of Michaelangelo's reclining tomb sculptures such as the *Aurora* from the Tomb of Lorenzo and the *Night* from the Tomb of Guiliano, both in the Medici Chapel. The derivation is used again in *Lycida* illustration to Milton (Schiff 903-906).

3. Fuseli categorized painting styles into three effective types based on their emotional expressiveness, the least expressive being history painting followed by the pathetic effect of dramatic painting. The highest order was epic painting which embodied the sublime. Dotson, p. 125.

25
Henry Fuseli, R.A.
English (born Switzerland) 1741-1825
Puck, ca. 1790
Oil on canvas, 36¼ x 28⅛
Folger Shakespeare Library, Washington, D.C.

This painting is a variation on a similar work made for the Boydell Gallery between 1787 and 1790, and published in the 1802 edition of *The Dramatic Works of Shakespeare.*[1] Puck, or Robin Goodfellow as he is also known in *A Midsummer Night's Dream,* is the fairy king Oberon's servant and messenger. He is plump and curly-haired, resembling a child, and accompanied by a diminutive fairy riding the back of a bee.[2] In keeping with Fuseli's theory of the sublime, Puck is simultaneously presented as a powerful creature of the imagination; a mischievious, sinister gremlin emerging from the darkness with potent magical ability. This impression is enhanced by his exaggerated posture, which suggests the speed with which he flies across the landscape. The Boydell painting (and the engraving derived from it) refer to Puck's description of himself in Act II, scene i: "I am that merry wanderer of the night..." and show among other details, a startled horse which illustrates his allusion to a beguiled "Bean-fed horse." This present variation contains none of this attendant detail and by increasing the smoke and mist surrounding the figure, Fuseli may have shifted the reference to Oberon's command in Act III, scene i: "The starry welkin cover thou anon/With drooping fog as black as Acheron." Some visual confusion arises from the fact that the Folger version was painted over an earlier work which is now faintly visible in the lower half of the painting.

Exhibitions: Washington, D.C.: *Shakespeare the Globe and the World* (traveling exhibition by the Folger Shakespeare Library) 1979-1981; Washington, D.C.: Federal Reserve Board, *According to Shakespeare: 18th and 19th Century English Painting,* 1976-1977 (no. 9)

References:

Samuel Schonebaum, *Shakespeare: The Globe and the World* (New York: The Folger Shakespeare Library and Oxford University Press, 1979) p. 155 illus

Gert Schiff, *Johann Heinrich Fussli* (Zurich: Schweizerisches Institute for Kunstwissenschaft, 1973) vol. I, p. 495 illus. vol. 2, p. 186

1. In *Robin Goodfellow-Puck* (Schiff 750), the work painted and engraved for Boydell, Fuseli reverses the positions of the figure's arms (the right holds the whip-like chain), endows him with wings, and cast his more demonic face further into shadow. Details visible below the figure on the ground, including the rearing horse referred to by Puck in Act II, scene i. A hazy atmosphere surrounds Puck in the Folger variation with a suggestion of rocks below. See Gert Schiff, *Johann Heinrich Fussli,* Zurich: Schweizerisches Institute for Kunstwisenshaft, 1973, p. 495, no. 750.

2. Fuseli shows the fairy riding on the back of a bee in another painting for the Boydell Gallery, *Titania Awakening* (1785-1790) (see fig. 6, Oakley essay) (Schiff 754). The figure in this context may represent Cobweb, who is asked by Bottom in act four, scene one to procure a "honey bag" from such a bee.

26 See Plate XI
John Gilbert, R.A.
English, 1817-1897
The Plays of William Shakespeare, 1849
Oil on canvas, 40⅜ x 50⅛
Signed and dated lower right: John Gilbert 1849
Mr. and Mrs. E. Hal Dickson, Mr. and Mrs. James R. Duncan and Mr. and Mrs. Frank W. Rose, San Angelo, Texas

John Gilbert's assembly of individual characters and vignettes from Shakespeare's plays "was a production of great power," wrote the *Art Journal* reviewer of 1850, with "every impersonation amply pronounced." The work is one of at least two such compilations by the prominent Victorian illustrator.[1]

The characters are arranged in a serpentine fashion, with some of the leading figures placed in the foreground: Lear curses his fate, Iago whispers to Othello, Shylock evades Portia and Hamlet broods above the melancholy Ophelia. Extending back onto a series of stonework terraces and into the rocky landscape are historical characters such as Henry VIII with Cardinal Wolsey and the comic figure of Falstaff in the laundry basket. The upper portion of the composition belongs to the supernatural beings: Puck, Ariel and Macbeth's witches. Apart from the general compositional references to Raphael's frescoes in the Stanze della Segnatura of the Vatican, the concept for the work reflects similar depictions of Shakespearean characters surrounding the playwright by early nineteenth-century artists such as Thomas Stothard and J. M. Wright.[2]

Gilbert was an accomplished illustrator, producing thousands of designs for popular periodicals such as *Punch* and the *Illustrated London News*. He executed prodigious numbers of Shakespearean subjects, both as illustrations for eighteen separate editions of the plays, and individual watercolor and oil painting for exhibition at the Royal Academy or Royal Water Colour Society.[3] He was an important factor in the rise of wood engraving; his own proficiency was such that he could draw directly on the wooden block without preliminary studies. His successful career was capped by his election to the Presidency of the Old Water Colour Society in 1871 and a knighthood, conferred by Queen Victoria in 1872.

Exhibition: London: The British Institution, 1850, no. 64

References:
The Art Journal, 1850, p. 89
Geoffrey Ashton, *Shakespeare and British Art* (New Haven: Yale Center for British Art, 1981) p. 20

1. A watercolor composition titled *Apotheosis of Shakespeare's Characters* (1871) is in the collection of the Yale Center for British Art. It is vertical rather than horizontal and compressed into a shallower space. A number of the characters represented are the same, but their positions relative to one another in the composition vary. Some of the characters show the same, or very similar, costumes, poses and gestures. The placement of the figures is circular within an arched format. Both demonstrate Gilbert's formula approach, in which he reused characteristic gestures, poses, etc., from composition to composition.

2. Ashton, p. 20.

3. One of Gilbert's best-known projects was the lavish illustration of *The Works of Shakespeare,* ed. Howard Staunton. *The Illustrations by John Gilbert Engraved by the Brothers Dalziel in three volumes.* London: Routledge, Warne and Routledge, Broadway, Ludgate Hill, 1864. He drew about twenty illustrations for each play to be integrated into the page layout for the text of the play itself rather than segregated as separate plates. He exhibited forty-five Shakespearean subjects at the Old Watercolor Society from 1852 to 1888, and six at the Royal Academy. Geoffrey Ashton, *Shakespeare's Heroines in the Nineteenth Century.* Buxton: Museum and Art Gallery, 1980, p.22.

27 See Plate XII
Maurice Greiffenhagen, R.A.
English, 1862-1931
Ophelia and Laertes, 1885
Oil on canvas, 50⅜ x 40
Signed and dated lower right: Maurice Greiffenhagen 1885
Mr. and Mrs. E. Hal Dickson, Mr. and Mrs. James R. Duncan, and Mr. and Mrs. Frank W. Rose, San Angelo, Texas

Many artists of the late nineteenth-century drew upon the popular contemporary interest in psychology in their depictions of Shakespearean characters. In this scene from *Hamlet*, the "mad" Ophelia is not merely a passive victim, but clearly exhibits the irrational behavior indicative of her mental state.[1]

The death of her father and her rejection by Hamlet have resulted in Ophelia's loss of reason, demonstrated by her nonsensical speech and singing. Her brother Laertes has just learned of their father's death from the King and Queen, and is horrified at the entrance of the raving Ophelia, who offers him some of the flowers and herbs with which she has become obsessed. The rigidity of Ophelia's body and her vacant expression declare her condition, and the reactions of the other characters—the King's stoicism, the Queen's anguished posture and Laertes' shocked stare—confirm the tragedy of her downfall.

Best known as an illustrator of books and magazines, Greiffenhagen exhibited with the New English Art Club, formed in 1886 as an alternative to the Royal Academy. (He was eventually elected to the Academy, later in his career, in 1922.) He was one of the youthful English followers of the French artist Jules Bastien-Lepage. The refined use of tonal harmonies and decorative motifs derived from medieval sources in *Ophelia and Laertes* reveal Greiffenhagen's attraction to the art of Bastien-Lepage. This painting is probably the "subject from Hamlet" which Greiffenhagen painted for the Royal Academy competition while in his final year at the Academy Schools.[2]

References:
Kenneth McConkey, "Listening to the Voices: A Study of Some Aspects of Jules Bastien-Lepage's 'Joan of Arc Listening to the Voices,'" *Art*, January, 1982, p. 154-158
Sadakichi Hartmann, *Shakespeare in Art*, (Boston: L. C. Paget, 1900) p. 290

1. See Kenneth McConkey, "Listening to the Voices: A Study of Some Aspects of Jules Bastien-Lepage's 'Joan of Arc Listening to the Voices,'" *Arts*, January, 1982, p. 158.

2. J. Stanley Little, "Maurice Greiffenhagen and His Work," *The Studio* IX, 46, (January, 1897) 239.

28
William Hamilton, R.A.
English, 1751-1801
Joan of Arc and the Furies
Oil on canvas, 30⅜ x 22
Purchase, The Betsy Mudge Wilson Memorial Fund,
Vassar College Art Gallery, Poughkeepsie, New York

Hamilton was the son of an architect associated with Robert Adam, who enabled the young artist to study in Italy with the painter Antonio Zucchi. He returned to London and the Royal Academy Schools in 1769. Hamilton made many book illustrations in addition to portraits and history paintings. In addition to his large contribution to the Boydell Gallery, he painted works for Woodmason's *Irish Shakespeare Gallery* and Bell's *British Theatre*.

This representation of Joan of Arc derives from the first part of *Henry VI*, where she is called Joan La Pucelle. It was among the twenty-three works Hamilton contributed to Alderman Boydell's *Shakespeare Gallery*, the collection commissioned to promote the development of history painting in England.[1]

Shakespeare's Joan is not the brave Maid of Orleans popularized in French legend, but is seen instead from the English point of view, a sorceress controlling demonic forces in the service of the French army. In the scene here depicted, Joan, on the brink of defeat, summons her friends, exhorting them to assist her in a last battle to save France. They refuse, and the painting illustrates her final speech of despair—"See, they forsake me? Now the time is come/ That France must vail her lofty-plumèd crest/ And let her head fall into England's lap./ My ancient incantations are too weak,/ And hell too strong for me to buckle with./ Now, France, thy glory droopeth to the dust." In keeping with the Neoclassic tradition, Joan resembles a figure of Bellona, goddess of war; a certain Fuselian influence appears in the fury of the wind and stormy sky and in the Michaelangelesque shapes of the grotesque spirits hovering in the darkness.

Exhibitions: London: Boydell's Shakespeare Gallery, 1795-1805; Detroit: Detroit Institute of Arts, *Romantic Art in Britain: Paintings and Drawings 1760-1860*, 1969 (no. 77); Santa Barbara: University Art Galleries, University of California, *William Blake and the Art of His Time*, 1976 (no. 52); Stratford, Ontario: The Gallery/Stratford, *Fantastic Shakespeare*, 1978 (no. 26)

References:
"Shakespeare Gallery" *The Lady's Monthly Museum*, vol. 15 (July 1805) p. 30 Thomas J. McCormick, *Vassar College Art Gallery, Selections from the Permanent Collection*, 1967, p. 25, illus. p. 130
Corlette Rossiter Walker, *William Blake in the Art of His Time*, Santa Barbara: University Art Galleries, 1976, cat. no. 52, illus. p. 59
David L. Shirey, "Romantic Art in Britain," *Antiques* 93 (April 1968) p. 501, illus. p. 501
Frederick Cummings and Allen Staley, *Romantic Art in Britain: Paintings and Drawings, 1760-1860*, Detroit: Detroit Institute of Arts, 1968, p. 136-7, illus. p. 136
Winifred H. Freidman, *Boydell's Shakespeare Gallery* (PhD Dissertation, Harvard University, 1974) New York: Garland Publishing Company, 1976, pp. 182-83, 224, illus. fig. 119
Vassar College Art Gallery: Paintings, 1300-1900, 1983, p. 121, illus. p. 121

---

1. Hamilton's *Joan of Arc and the Furies* was engraved by Anker Smith, first published 1 January 1795 as "First Part of King Henry VI, act V, scene iiii; Joan La Pucelle and Friends," and again, in 1802, for *The Dramatic Works of Shakespeare*.

29
William Hamilton, R.A.
English, 1751-1801
Gloucester's Murderer Denounced
Oil on canvas, 106¼ x 82
Bob Jones University, Greenville, South Carolina

In a highly theatrical presentation, Hamilton recreates the confrontation over the dead body of the Duke of Gloucester in *King Henry VI, Part II.* The Duke of Warwick gestures dramatically at the dead Gloucester as he accuses Suffolk of the murder. Suffolk draws his sword in threatened retaliation, as the young King (seated in the foreground) mourns his uncle's death. The Queen, shown beside her ally Suffolk, denies Warwick's charges. Suffolk's conspirator, Cardinal Beaufort, slips out of the room, betraying his guilt with a shifty look over the shoulder.

Hamilton enjoyed a substantial reputation as a history painter in the manner of Joshua Reynolds. Among his portraits were many of theatrical figures, and he sometimes incorporated portraits of his actor friends into his historical scenes.[1] Sarah Siddons was a frequent subject—his portrait of her as *Isabella, with Her Son* (1782, unlocated) was a great public success which led to his being named an Associate of the Royal Academy in 1784. Hamilton was elevated to Academician following the exhibition of his *J. P. Kemble as Richard III* in 1788.[2]

The 'death bed scene' was a fixture of later eighteenth-century history painting.[3] One of Reynold's Boydell paintings was a *Death of Cardinal Beaufort* (fig. 7 Oakley essay) from the same play, *Henry VI, Part II.* The eclectic costumes in the present painting follow the fashion of those found in contemporary theatrical productions. The costumes and highly dramatic treatment in *Gloucester's Murderer Denounced* suggest the influence of theatrical productions upon Hamilton's depiction of this subject.

1. A. T. Spanton, "William Hamilton, R.A." The *Connoisseur,* 21 (1908) 37.

2. C. Reginald Grundy, "William Hamilton, R.A." *The Connoisseur,* 72 (1925) 203.

3. See Robert Rosenblum, *Transformations in Late Eighteenth-Century Art* (Princeton: Princeton University Press, 1967).

30
George Henry Harlow
English, 1787-1819
Mrs. Siddons as Lady Macbeth
Oil on canvas, 94½ x 58
Bob Jones University, Greenville, South Carolina

As the critic Charles Lamb wrote in 1811, "We speak of Lady Macbeth, while we are in reality thinking of Mrs. S."[1] "Mrs. S." was Sarah Siddons, a member of the famous Kemble family of actors, and perhaps history's most influential interpreter of the part. She was widely praised for the depth of her psychological insight into the woman who destroys her husband by goading him into murder. She possessed an uncanny ability to inspire terror and dread in her audiences, and much of her innovative stage business became standard in later performances.

Mrs. Siddons as Lady Macbeth is one of two standing, full-length portraits of the actress in that role painted by Harlow.[2] She holds the letter received by Lady Macbeth from her husband in Act I, scene v, recounting his meeting with the witches and their prophecy that he would one day be King of Scotland. Her steady gaze suggests her inward resolve as she considers the implication of the prophecy: if Macbeth is to be king, then Duncan must die. The low vantage point of this work sends Siddons towering above the viewer, conveying the power and immense stage presence she is reputed to have projected in life.[3]

Harlow was a painter of theatrical portraits and historical subjects. After some five years of training with various teachers including Thomas Lawrence, he became a professional artist in 1805 at the age of 17. Harlow painted a number of Shakespearean theatrical portraits, mostly derived from his association with the Kemble Family. Among these were *Charles Kemble as Hubert in 'King John'* (unlocated) and *The Trial Scene from Henry VIII* (ca. 1817, Trustees of the Morrison Picture Settlement, England) featuring Siddons as Queen Katherine, which received great acclaim at the Royal Academy in 1817.

Exhibition: London: The Art Council, *Shakespeare in Art*, 1964 (no. 44)

Reference:
Arts Council of Great Britain, *Shakespeare in Art* (London: Arts Council of Great Britain, 1964) pp. 23-24

1. Quoted in Esther Gordon Dotson, *Shakespeare Illustrated, 1770-1820* (PhD Dissertation, New York University, 1973) p. 135.

2. This work is a larger version of a painting (23¼ x 14½) in the Garrick Club. The Bob Jones version may have been painted for Robert Arkwright, who was related to the Kembles by marriage. Either this version or the Garrick's smaller one was engraved by C. Rolls as a frontispiece to the Literary Souvenir, 1830. A second painting of Mrs. Siddons in the role of Lady Macbeth from Act V, scene i (the so-called Sleepwalking scene) is in the Garrick Club. See C. K. Adams, *A Catalogue of Pictures in the Garrick Club* (London: The Garrick Club, 1936) nos. 31 and 43.

3. The low viewpoint was probably inspired by Lawrence's portrait of John Philip Kemble as Coriolanus (fig. 11 Oakley essay).

31
Thomas Hicks, N.A.
American, 1823-1890
Edwin Booth as Iago, 1863
Oil on canvas, 31½ x 21½
Signed and dated lower right: T. Hicks 1863
National Portrait Gallery,
Smithsonian Institution, Washington, D.C.,
Transfer from the Cooper-Hewitt Museum of Decorative Arts, Gift of Miss Charlotte Arnold, 1920.

This portrait captures the stage presence as well as the likeness of Edwin Booth, who, with malevolent frown and defiant stance, confronts the viewer in the role of the wicked Iago. A scion of one of America's premier acting families, Booth was especially acclaimed for his Shakespearean roles, which included Hamlet and Richard III as well as Iago.

This painting is a replica of a larger work now in The Players, New York, cut down from its original life-size. It evidently shows the actor at the culmination of the first scene in the fifth act after Iago has orchestrated the murder of Roderigo.[1] With this murder, Iago sets into motion his plan to destroy Othello. His calculating cruelty is expressed in the actor's nervous wariness and burning eyes as he observes the results of his scheming from a doorway. The costume cannot be identified with any known to have been worn by Booth as Iago during the 1860s and 70s; but the painting may document his appearance in a specific performance.[2]

Thomas Hicks, a first cousin of the American primitive painter Edward Hicks, studied at the National Academy and the Pennsylvania Academy before completing his training in Thomas Couture's studio in Paris. His tight, minutely detailed approach to painting assured his reputation as a portraitist. He was elected to the National Academy in 1851.

Exhibitions: Washington: National Portrait Gallery, *Portraits of the American Stage,* 1971 (no. 23); Stratford, Ontario: The Gallery/Stratford, *Fantastic Shakespeare* 1978 (no. 30)

Reference:

National Portrait Gallery, *Portraits of the American Stage, 1771-1971,* Washington: Smithsonian Institution Press, 1971, p. 60, illus. frontispiece

1. A second small study is in the Players and a third is unlocated. The attribution of the composition to Act V, scene i is made in unattributed newspaper accounts contemporary to the original work. These accounts are in the scrapbook of Mrs. Thomas Hicks in the files of the National Portrait Gallery, Washington, D.C.

2. One contemporary account of the portrait (see note above) states "Our readers who have seen the performer in his play (e.g. 'Othello') will recall his picturesque dress, his graceful attitude and his cynical look..." In 1862 and 63 Booth was performing at the Winter Garden Theatre in New York.

32
Robert Alexander Hillingford
English, 1828-1904
Othello Recounting His Adventures to Desdemona, 1869
Oil on canvas, 19½ x 28½
Signed in monogram and dated lower left: 18 RH 69
Mr. and Mrs. E. Hal Dickson, Mr. and Mrs. James R. Duncan, Mr. and Mrs. Frank W. Rose, San Angelo, Texas

A production of splendid effect, with attention to historical accurate detail, was the goal of nineteenth-century stage designers and artists alike. This scene from Shakespeare's *Othello* reflects an antiquarian's interest in period costume and props, all sumptuously painted in a style strongly influenced by the great sixteenth-century Venetian masters.

In Act I, scene iii of the play, Othello, a Moorish general in the service of the Venetian state, describes his visits to the home of Senator Brabantio. On these occasions the Senator's daughter Desdemona was captivated by the general's recital of his military exploits. As Othello spoke "of most disastrous chances of moving accidents by flood and field" Desdemona was moved to pity, and later to marry the Moor against her father's will. Hillingford conveys the martial tone of Shakespeare's poetry by showing Othello in armor displaying the torn battle standards as Desdemona and her father follow his tale with rapt attention. Hillingford invents an interior filled with sixteenth-century furniture, textiles and other objects. Both Desdemona and Othello are surrounded by props which emphasize the disparity in their conditions: the gentle, domestic Desdemona by delicate Venetian glass and a lute; Othello by the armor and trophies of war. The sumptuous fabrics, clear-toned color and the expansion of the shallow foreground into the open sky beyond the balcony are reminiscent of Venetian master, Paolo Veronese.

Robert Alexander Hillingford exhibited history and literary subjects, primarily at the Royal Academy, between 1864 and 1902. He built an impressive collection of armor and antiques and used them repeatedly in his paintings. His style reflects his study in Germany, at the Munich and Dusseldorf academies, and especially a long period of residence in Italy. He also painted subjects from *The Taming of the Shrew, The Two Gentlemen of Verona,* and *The Merchant of Venice,* all "Italian" plays.

Exhibition: Buxton, Derbyshire: Buxton Museum, *Shakespeare's Heroines of the 19th Century,* 1980 (no. 13)

References:

F. Gordon Roe, "The Hillingford Saga," *The Connoisseur,* II (September 1975) pp. 50-55

Geoffrey Ashton, *Shakespeare's Heroines in the 19th Century,* Buxton, Derbyshire; Derbyshire Museum Service, 1980, p. 30, illus. p. 31

33   See Plate XIII
Edward Robert Hughes, R.W.S.
English, 1851-1914
The Shrew Katherina, 1896
Watercolor and bodycolor on paper, 28 x 19
Signed and dated, lower right: E R Hughes 1896
Mr. and Mrs. E. Hal Dickson, Mr. and Mrs. James R. Duncan, and Mr. and Mrs. Frank W. Rose, San Angelo, Texas

Edward Robert Hughes, who was the nephew of the Pre-Raphaelite follower Arthur Hughes and a student of Holman Hunt, was strongly influenced by the Brotherhood's meticulous approach to representation. In *The Shrew Katherina* he is less concerned with illustrating Shakespeare's story than with reproducing in minute detail Katherine's splendid brocade costume, the ornate furniture, and the richly textured objects surrounding her. Hughes' Katherine is not the shrill shrew of previous decades (see cat. nos. 7 and 20)—the emphasis has shifted from narrative to decorative in this work saturated with the introspective mood of the English Aesthetic Movement.

The single female figure, depicted in abstracted reverie and surrounded by an assortment of symbolic props (here an empty plate and glass, which refer to Katherine's hunger) was a favorite motif of artists of the Aesthetic Movement such as Dante Gabriel Rossetti, Albert Moore, and Edward Burne-Jones. They directed their attention toward the artful placement of the compositional elements and the subtle manipulation of tonal color harmonies—an abstract and decorative rather than literal approach.

34
Charles Hunt
English, 1803-1877
My 'Macbeth', 1863
Oil on canvas, 19⅞ x 26
Signed and dated lower right: C. Hunt 1863
The FORBES Magazine Collection, New York

Charles Hunt specialized in charming compositions showing costumed children parodying adult situations. Such a work is the center of attention in *My 'Macbeth'*, a self-portrait of the artist with his wife and son. The positive reviews received by *The Banquet Scene, Macbeth* when it was exhibited at the Royal Academy in 1864 may have been a factor in the apparent pleasure and pride with which the artist draws attention to the painting.[1]

Hunt reproduces with meticulous precision a middle-class Victorian parlour and its eminently respectable inhabitants. Their grave demeanor is somewhat mitigated, however, by the slightly ridiculous quality of the painting on the easel. Hunt's own gesture is echoed by the preposterously costumed children, who point back at him in a mocking way. Although relatively little is known of the details of Hunt's career, his work closely parallels that of Thomas Webster and F. D. Hardy, two of Hunt's contemporaries of the Cranbrook colony.[2]

Hunt exhibited at the Royal Academy from 1862, and at the British Institution and the Society of British Artists. He is known to have painted two other humorous pictures of children enacting scenes from Shakespeare, *The Play Scene from 'Hamlet'* (Yale Center for British Art, New Haven), also in 1863, and *The Trial Scene, Merchant of Venice* in 1868. His repeated use of Shakespearean subjects is indicative of their popularity and their pervasiveness in the art of nineteenth century.

Exhibitions: London: M. Newman Ltd., *The Victorian Scene*, 1962; Minneapolis: University Gallery, University of Minnesota, *The Art and Mind of Victorian England: Paintings from the Forbes Magazine Collection*, 1974 (no. 23); New York: Metropolitan Museum of Art, *The Royal Academy Revisited (1837-1901)*, 1975 (no. 29)

References:

Mario Amaya, "Nineteenth Century Art: The Opening Vista," *Apollo*, December, 1962, p. 807

Melvin Waldfogel, "Introduction," *The Art and Mind of Victorian England: Paintings from the Forbes Magazine Collection*, Minneapolis: University Gallery University of Minnesota, 1974, p. 19

Christopher Forbes, *The Royal Academy Revisited 1837-1901*, (New York: The Forbes Collection, 1975) p. 74

1. The copy of the *Art Journal* which lies on the chair in the foreground was apparently added after that magazine published its favorable review in 1864. See Christopher Forbes *The Royal Academy Revisited 1837-1901* (New York: The Forbes Collection, 1975) p. 74.

2. See Graham Reynolds, *Victorian Painting* (New York: The Macmillan Company, 1906) p. 36. The Cranbrook Colony was a group of artists who resided and painted in Kent.

35
William Knight Keeling
English, 1807-1886
Touchstone, Audrey and William
Oil on panel, 27¼ x 33½
Mr. and Mrs. E. Hal Dickson, Mr. and Mrs. James R. Duncan and Mr. and Mrs. Frank W. Rose, San Angelo, Texas

Three characters derived from the pastoral tradition in stage comedy are featured in this scene. Audrey, the shepherdess standing to the left, is the object of both Touchstone and Shepherd William's affections and listens shyly as the Clown threatens his rival with harm in every conceivable fashion. William appears dumbfounded as he attempts to comprehend the verbal assault, but will eventually leave peacefully, befuddled by Touchstone's agile tongue and ready wit. Audrey and William wear the stage dress prescribed for pastoral characters and Touchstone the motley of the clown.

William Knight Keeling was an illustrator and portrait painter active in the art circles of Manchester after 1835. He continued to exhibit many watercolors and some oil paintings in London, showing this work at the Royal Academy in 1855. Keeling's handling of the oil medium, which is applied in thin washes, may reflect his practice as watercolorist.

Exhibition: London: The Royal Academy, 1855 (no. 1277)

36
Frederic Leighton, P.R.A.
English, 1830-1896
Oil study for *Desdemona*
Oil on canvas, 21½ x 18
Leighton House, London

Frederic Leighton was one of the preeminent English artists of the late nineteenth-century, a painter of historical and literary subjects who was elected President of the Royal Academy in 1878. He painted several scenes from Shakespeare's plays, the earliest ones such as *The Reconciliation of the Montagues and the Capulets over the Dead Bodies of Romeo and Juliet* (1853-55, Agnes Scott College, Decatur, Georgia; fig. 23 Oakley essay) demonstrating the medievalizing tendencies of his early training.

In 1888 the *Graphic* magazine commissioned a series of 21 paintings of Shakespeare's heroines, each to be depicted by a different artist.[1] The present painting is an oil study for Leighton's contribution, a portrait of Desdemona. During the 1860s Leighton abandoned the archaizing, medievalizing style he had adopted during his studies in Berlin and Florence and developed a more painterly, sensuous one derived from Italian Renaissance art. The Italian Desdemona, dressed in opulent Renaissance fashion, is similar to the beautiful women in classical costume, executed in delicate tonal harmonies, which were the artist's favorite subjects in his later years.

Reference:
Leonée and Richard Ormond. *Lord Leighton.* New Haven: Yale University Press for the Paul Mellon Centre for Studies in British Art, 1975, p. 170

---

1. Geoffrey Ashton, *Shakespeare's Heroines in the Nineteenth Century,* Buxton: The Museum and Art Gallery, 1980 p. iv.

37
Charles Robert Leslie, R.A.
English (born America) 1794-1859
Katherine of Aragon with Her Maid, 1826
Oil on canvas, 22½ x 19½
Royal Academy of Arts, London

American C. R. Leslie was renowned in England for his compositions derived from literary sources such as Cervantes, Molière, Goldsmith and Shakespeare. His paintings combine the two trends which had predominated in the depiction of Shakespearean subjects for over a century—the historical and the theatrical. Leslie habitually avoided the dramatic, sublime interpretations of the previous generation and chose episodes with a powerful contemplative or narrative element.

Through Washington Allston, a fellow American who was one of his earliest acquaintances in London, Leslie met poet and Shakespearean critic Samuel Taylor Coleridge, who may have encouraged his interest in Shakespearean subjects as he had Allston's earlier. Leslie's devotion to the source is apparent from the number of Shakespearean paintings and studies he produced utilizing many different plays.[1] As a devotee of the theatre, Leslie was most certainly inspired by Sarah Siddons' performances in the role of Queen Katherine to choose this character as the subject for several paintings, including this 1826 version which was his Diploma painting for the Royal Academy.[2]

Leslie grew up in Philadelphia and studied there briefly with Thomas Sully.[3] He went to London to continue his studies in 1811, and elected to remain there for most of the rest of his life. In later life he published two important books on art, the first a life of the painter John Constable, and in 1855, his "Handbook for Young Painters."

Exhibitions: London: The Royal Academy, 1842 (no. 148); London: The Royal Academy, 1951 (no. 268); London: The Arts Council of Great Britain, *British Subject and Narrative Pictures,* 1955 (no. 23); Bournemouth: 1957; Nottingham: Nottingham University, *Victorian Painting,* 1959 (no. 40); London: The Arts Council, 1961 (no. 22); London: The Royal Academy, 1963 (no. 202); Belfast: Ulster Museum, *Shakespeare Themes,* 1964 (no. 24); Buxton: Buxton Museum and Art Gallery, *Shakespeare's Heroines in the Nineteenth Century,* 1980 (no. 16).

References:

C. R. Leslie, *Autobiographical Recollections,* 1869, p. 166
Geoffrey Ashton, *Shakespeare's Heroines in the Nineteenth Century,* Buxton: The Buxton Museum and Art Gallery, 1980, p. 36, illus.
Sadakichi Hartmann, *Shakespeare in Art,* Boston: L. C. Paget, 1900, pp. 117-121

1. Leslie's Shakespearean subjects include *Flouzel and Perdita* (1837, Victoria and Albert), *Hermione* (1856, Royal Shakespeare Theatre Gallery, Stratford-on-Avon) *Viola and Olivia* (1859, Tate Gallery) and *Slender, with the Assistance of Shallow, Courting Anne Page* (ca. 1825, Yale Center for British Art.).

2. Geoffrey Ashton, *Shakespeare's Heroines in the Nineteenth Century* (Buxton: Buxton Museum and Art Gallery, 1980) p. 36. Leslie painted Queen Katherine for John Sheepshanks in 1842, this version now at the Victoria and Albert. A third work is Queen Catherine of Aragon's Interview *with Capucius...* at the Mead Art Museum, Amherst College.

3. Robin Hamlyn in his forthcoming monograph on the artist states that several of the early drawings by the artist exhibited in Philadelphia were of the English actor George Frederick Cooke as Richard III. These were produced at the same time as Sully's painting of the actor (cat. no. 60).

38
Emanuel Leutze
American (born Germany) 1816-1868
The Merry Wives of Windsor, 1865
Oil on canvas, 30⅛ x 40⅛
Signed and dated, lower left: E. Leutze 1865
Corcoran Gallery of Art, Gift of Mr. and
Mrs. Lloyd E. Raport

Emanuel Leutze, a narrative and history painter trained largely at the Academy in Dusseldorf, painted this light-hearted scene from Shakespeare's *Merry Wives of Windsor* in the United States, late in his career. Although Leutze painted many representations of subjects from English Tudor and Republican history in a similar vein, this is his only depiction of a theatrical scene.

In this episode the play's two scheming wives, Mrs. Ford and Mrs. Page, watch with apparent amusement as two servants spirit their old antagonist, the knight John Falstaff, out of Mrs. Ford's home in a basket of dirty laundry. The ruse is necessitated by the arrival of Mrs. Ford's husband, who suspects that the knight is conducting a secret romance with the ladies and stops the frightened servants to question them. The floor is littered with discarded linen, a reminder of the sense of urgency with which Falstaff was secreted in the basket. Above Ford's head is a pair of antlers, and on the stair landing a tapestry depicting a fleeing man with horns. Both allude to the buck's horns mentioned in the play as a symbol of cuckholdry and presage the final scene at Herne's Oak when Falstaff, similarly horned, learns he is the object of the wives' deception.

Leutze was born in Schwabisch-Gmund, Germany, in 1816, and emigrated at age nine with his family to Philadelphia. He worked for a time as an itinerant portraitist in Virginia, Maryland, and Pennsylvania before travelling to Dusseldorf in 1841. He spent most of his career in Europe, where he executed many Academic history paintings including the well-known *Washington Crossing the Delaware* (1850, The Metropolitan Museum of Art).

Exhibition: Washington, D.C.: Corcoran Gallery of Art, *Acquisitions Since 1975*, 1982-83.

Reference:

Barbara S. Groseclose, *Emanuel Leutze, 1816-1868: Freedom is the Only King*, Washington: Smithsonian Institution Press, 1975, p. 101, no. 120 illus.

39
Edwin Long
English, 1829-1891
Henry Irving as Richard, Duke of Gloucester, 1877
Oil on canvas, 57⅜ x 40
Signed and dated in monogram lower left: 18 EL 77
Bob Jones University, Greenville, SC

That Shakespeare's *Richard III* played a key role in building many theatrical reputations is demonstrated by the number of great actors portrayed in the part.[1] Among them was Henry Irving, the premier late nineteenth-century interpreter of Shakespeare's tragic characters. In this portrait by Edwin Long, Irving assumes his stage identity as Richard without reference to any specific scene while suggesting the psychological complexity of the part.

Edwin Long was best known as a painter of exotic subjects derived from ancient Egypt, Rome and the Near East. He was also a friend and traveling companion of Irving's, and must have had a first-hand knowledge of the actor in this role. Irving is shown standing before a backdrop painted with flowers and animals, wearing an elaborate costume with jewel-encrusted belt, chain and a fur cloak. Irving was renowned for the subtlety of his characterizations, suggested by Long in the portrait's hooded eyes, thin mouth and nervous hands.

Born John Henry Brodribb in 1838, Irving made his London debut at the St. James Theatre in 1866. He built his reputation on the Shakespearean roles of Hamlet, Othello and Macbeth, and around the time this portrait was made had entered into a partnership with the actress Ellen Terry that would last until 1902.

Exhibition: London: Royal Academy Exhibition 1878 (no. 472)

References:

Shakespeareana; Paintings, Drawings, and Ceramics. Property of the American Shakespeare Theatre, Stratford (auction catalogue) Sotheby Park-Bernet, January 15, 1976, no. 130 illus.

The National Portrait Gallery, *Portraits of the American Stage,* Washington: Smithsonian Press, 1971, p. 72, illus.

---

1. Among the portraits of actors in the role of Richard are three of David Garrick: one by Hogarth (1746) a second by Hayman (1760) and a third by Dance-Holland (1771) (cat. no. 15) John Neagle painted Edmund Kean as Richard around 1826 (cat. no. 46) and Sully depicted George Frederick Cooke in the role in 1811 (cat. no. 60).

40
Daniel Maclise, R.A.
English, 1806-1870
The Play Scene from 'Hamlet', 1842
Oil on canvas, 20 x 36
Signed and dated lower left: D. Maclise 1842
Mr. and Mrs. E. Hal Dickson, Mr. and Mrs. James R. Duncan and Mr. and Mrs. Frank W. Rose, San Angelo, Texas

The original version of this work, now in the Tate Gallery, London, was the sensation of the Royal Academy exhibition of 1842. One of the most important theatrical paintings of the century, it was instrumental in establishing Maclise's reputation. This copy is approximately one-third the size of the original, which measures 60 x 108 inches, and was commissioned by Thomas G. Williams in the early 1860s.[1]

Hamlet, Prince of Denmark, has laid a trap for his uncle, King Claudius, who is suspected of murdering Hamlet's father, the King of Denmark, in order to usurp the throne. On the stage, actors recreate the murder of a sleeping king. The murderer places poison in the king's ear as he greedily clutches the crown. The members of the audience observe the tableau, with the exception of Claudius who grips his hands convulsively and turns away from this accusation of guilt, and Ophelia, who lowers her head to observe Hamlet at her feet.

The central theme of the work is the opposition of the forces of good and evil. Maclise places Hamlet at the apex of an inverted pyramid, with Claudius, Gertrude and Polonius ranged on one side and Ophelia and Horatio on the other. In the background, above each group, are allegorical emblems—Ophelia sits directly beneath a statue with folded hands representing Prayer; a figure of Justice with sword and scales looms over the guilty Claudius. Biblical tapestries, the temptation and expulsion of Adam and Eve from the Garden to the left, and the murder and sacrifice of Abel to the right, refer to the play's themes of disinheritance and death. The enactment of the murder is placed in the center within a recessed archway and represents for the viewer a second, separate level of drama from that of the main characters. The ominous shadows cast by the players enhance the sense of theatricality. The reclining figure of Hamlet, whose form echoes that of the victim on stage, provides the compositional and thematic center of reference.[2] Reviewers' comments ranged from acclaiming it as "the lion of the gallery" and "the chef d'oeuvre of the British School" to John Ruskin's dismissal of it as a "grinning and glittering fantasy."

Maclise's iconographic source for *The Play Scene...* was a book of drawings titled *Outlines to Shakespeare* by the German artist Moritz Retzsch. He incorporated elements of Retzch's illustration of the play scene and his frontispiece to the outlines in choosing the allegorical references.[3] He also may have consulted lithographs by Eugene Deveria and Louis Boulanger (these based on Charles Kemble's performances in Paris in 1847),[4] but it was the Germanic influence which predominated in Maclise's art at the time, with its strong graphic quality and Gothic flavor.

After early training at the Cork School of Art, Maclise left Ireland in 1827 to study at the Royal Academy Schools in London. He had come to public attention first in Ireland with a drawing of Sir Walter Scott done in 1825, lithographed and widely distributed. He was recognized in London as a sensitive portraitist, well connected in literary circles. From 1830 to 1838 he executed a series of portraits of literary figures (among them his friend Charles Dickens) for *Fraser's Magazine*. His debut work at the Academy's annual exhibition of 1829, *Malvolio Affecting the Count,* was the first of many Shakespearean subjects Maclise painted early in his career. *The Play Scene...* was preceded by *Macbeth and the Weird Sisters* (ca. 1832, location unknown) *The Disenchantment of Bottom* (cat. no. 42), *A Scene from Twelfth Night* (ca. 1840, The Tate Gallery) and *The Banquet Scene in Macbeth* (1840, The Guildhall Art Gallery). Maclise chose historical subjects in his later career, and painted several frescoes for the redecoration of the Houses of Parliament. The last years of his life were dominated by the labor of painting two of these, *Wellington and Blucher* and *The Death of Nelson*, begun in 1857 and not completed until 1865.

Reference:

Arts Council of Great Britain, *Daniel Maclise 1806-1870*, London: Arts Council of Great Britain, 1972, p. 72

---

1. There are two watercolor replicas of the *Play Scene...*, one by Maclise now in the Forbes Collection, New York, and second by Alice Bolton, in the Royal Shakespeare Gallery, Stratford-on-Avon. The present work is that referred to in The Arts Council of Great Britain, *Daniel Maclise 1806-1870*, exhibition catalogue by Richard Ormond (London: The Arts Council of Great Britain, 1972) p. 72. Thomas G. Williams also commissioned a replica, presently untraced, of Maclise's *Banquet Scene in Macbeth*.

2. Christopher Forbes, *The Royal Academy Revisited 1837-1901* (New York: The Forbes Collection, 1975) p. 102. T. S. R. Boase in his article "Illustrations of Shakespeare's Plays in the Seventeenth and Eighteenth Centuries," *Journal of the Warburg and Courtauld Institute*, 10, 1947, p. 24, plate a, reproduces an engraving after Francis Hayman of the play scene from *Hamlet* which also utilizes the devices of background sculptural figures in niches.

3. *The Arts Council of Great Britain, Daniel Maclise 1806-1870*, p. 72.

4. Forbes, p. 102.

41
Daniel Maclise, R.A.
English, 1806-1870
King Lear and Cordelia
Oil on canvas, 18 x 24
Signed lower right: D Maclise
Mr. and Mrs. E. Hal Dickson, Mr. and Mrs. James R. Duncan and Mr. and Mrs. Frank W. Rose, San Angelo, Texas

The reconciliation of Lear and Cordelia occurs soon after the mad King has been found wandering on the heath in a violent storm. The emotional upheaval of the storm scene made it a popular subject for painters of Fuseli's generation, but Maclise's choice of the more sentimental aftermath is characteristic of the Victorian period.

Cordelia's arm, shoulders and head serve as a frame for the head of her father, whose ravaged face emerges from the dark background. The chiaroscuro reveals the pathetic character of the king's face and hands and also emphasizes the solidity of his daughter's body upon which he leans for support. Cordelia's elaborate hairstyle, and the color of her costume balance the composition although her face is only partially visible.

42
Daniel Maclise, R.A.
English, 1806-1870
The Disenchantment of Bottom, 1832
Oil on canvas, 50 x 40
The Ella Gallup Sumner and Mary Catlin Sumner Collection, Wadsworth Atheneum, Hartford, Connecticut

This painting depicts the moment when Puck releases Bottom from the spell cast by Oberon that turned the gentle simpleton into an ass. Maclise conceives of Bottom's disenchantment as a shocking experience—he cries out as he plummets through a whirling, cavernous space filled with malevolent fairies.

One of Maclise's earliest commissions was a series of illustrations for an edition of Crofton Croker's *Fairy Legends of Ireland,* 1826, and he painted pictures uniting elements of horror and fantasy.[1] His supernatural creatures hark back to those of Henry Fuseli in their weird configurations and leering countenances, and they anticipate the works of later fairy painters such as Richard Dadd (cat. no. 14) and Joseph Noel Paton.

Exhibitions: London: The Royal Academy, 1832 (no. 464); London: The British Institution, 1833 (no. 511); International Exhibition, 1862; Stratford-on-Avon: "Tercentenary of the Birth of Shakespeare," 1864 (no. 222)

References:
W. Justin O'Driscoll, *A Memoir of Daniel Maclise,* London: Longmans, Green & Co., 1871, p. 45
W. G. Strickland, *A Dictionary of Irish Artists,* vol. II, 1913, p. 66
Richard L. Ormond, "Daniel Maclise" *Burlington Magazine,* 110, (1968) p. 692

1. Richard Ormond, "Daniel Maclise" *Burlington Magazine,* 110, 1968, p. 690 notes two works in the fantastic vein which parallel the *Disenchantment...* They are *Mokanna Revealing his features to Zelica* (1883, Royal Academy) from Moore's *Lalla Rookh* and *Macbeth and the Weird Sisters* (1836, Royal Academy). In this article the present painting is catalogued as *Puck Disenchanting Bottom,* a study for which was listed in the artist's sale at Christie's, 24 June 1870 (no. 68).

43 See Plate XIV
Henry Stacy Marks, R.A., R.W.S.
English, 1829-1898
Bardolph, 1853
Oil on canvas, 21 x 17
Signed in monogram and dated lower left:
hsm 1853
Mr. and Mrs. E. Hal Dickson, Mr. and Mrs. James R.
Duncan and Mr. and Mrs. Frank W. Rose, San Angelo,
Texas

Falstaff's lieutenant Bardolph is a faithful retainer whose love of gambling, brawling and especially tippling are all apparent in Marks characterization. Bardolph is distinguished among Falstaff's ruffians by his face, which is "all bubukles, and whelks, and knobs and flames of fire" in testimony to his drinking habits. The carved insignia on his chair back indicates that he is at the rogue band's headquarters, The Boar's Head Tavern, Eastcheap, where he stares forlornly into a presumably empty jug.

Marks exhibited this work and his *Dogberry Examining Conrade and Borachio* in successive years at the Royal Academy shortly after his return from France where he studied with Picot. A watercolorist and illustrator, Marks was primarily known for his often humorous paintings of birds. The strong, even illumination and the sharp detail in Marks' paintings suggest his interest in the style of the Pre-Raphaelites, but his decidedly light-hearted approach distinguishes his work from the serious historicism of the members of the Brotherhood. Marks was affiliated with the St. John's Wood Clique, and was known for practical jokes and high spirits.

Exhibition: London: Royal Academy, 1854 (no. 1270)

44
Henry Stacy Marks, R.A., R.W.S.
English, 1829-1898
Dogberry Examining Conrade and Borachio, 1852
Oil on canvas, 21 x 17
Signed in monogram and dated lower right: hsm/1852
Mr. and Mrs. E. Hal Dickson, Mr. and Mrs. James R.
Duncan and Mr. and Mrs. Frank W. Rose, San Angelo,
Texas

Shakespeare's Constable Dogberry is an upright and conscientious fellow who covers his bumbling ineptitude in a sea of illogic and malapropisms. Yet it is his humorous examination of the two "false knaves" Conrade and Borachio, which reveals the intrigue to discredit Hero, and thus resolves the plot of "Much Ado About Nothing."[1]

Exhibition: London: Royal Academy Exhibition, 1853 (no. 538).

Reference:
G. C. Williamson, *Bryan's Dictionary*, vol. 3, London: Kennikat Press, 1964, p. 287

---

1. Sadakicki Hartmann in his book *Shakespeare in Art* (Boston: L. C. Paget, 1900) p. 198 mentions a painting by Marks entitled "Dogberrys Charge to the Watch" which could refer to this work.

45
William Mulready, R.A.
English (born Ireland) 1786-1863
Portrait of Othello
Oil on canvas, 15 15/16 x 11¾
Francis D. Murnaghan, Jr., Baltimore, Maryland

William Mulready was a child prodigy, admitted to the schools of the Royal Academy at the age of fourteen. He was elected an associate of the Academy in 1815 and to full membership in the following year. He enjoyed a long and very successful career as a painter of genre, contemporary life and literary subjects.

The present work demonstrates Mulready's masterful use of color, which he applied in clear glazes on a light ground. For this reason he is sometimes identified as a forerunner of the Pre-Raphaelites.[1] Between 1836 and 1838 he produced an ambitious Shakespearean painting, *The Seven Ages of Man* from *As You Like It*, which was reproduced in wood engraving as a frontispiece to the *Illustrations of Shakespeare's Seven Ages*, published in 1840.[2] Mulready used several black models, especially in the late 1850s and early 60s when he was preparing *The Toyseller*, an unfinished work in the National Gallery of Ireland.[3]

Exhibitions: Baltimore: The Walters Art Gallery, *African Image: Representations of the Black Throughout History*, 1980; Baltimore: The Walters Art Gallery, *An Irish Perspective*, 1983

---

1. Graham Reynolds, *Victorian Paintings*, New York: The Macmillan Company, 1966, p. 12.

2. Kathryn Moore Heleniak, *William Mulready*, New Haven: Yale University Press, 1980, pp. 213-214.

3. Heleniak, p. 221.

46
John Neagle
American, 1796-1865
Edmund Kean as Richard III
Oil on canvas, 26 x 22
Hampden-Booth Theatre Library, The Players, New York

Philadelphian John Neagle was largely self-trained, receiving only brief instruction from Bass Otis (1784-1861). Neagle established his reputation with a depiction of America's foremost portraitist, Gilbert Stuart (1825, National Society of Pennsylvania). That portrait and Neagle's *Pat Lyon at the Forge* (1826, Boston Museum of Fine Arts) are considered two of his finest works.

In 1826 he received a commission to paint a series of sixteen actor portraits, among them this depiction of the outstanding British actor Edmund Kean as Richard III.[1] The first sitting for the work took place at a New York dinner party where Kean, donning his costume, managed to call up his interpretation of the part by fortifying himself with great quantities of brandy.[2]

Kean was a talented and temperamental actor who won great fame for his interpretations of the principal tragic roles from Shakespeare. He had first come to the notice of London audiences with his portrayal of Shylock at Drury Lane in January, 1814. He was especially renowned as Richard III, and opened his engagement at the Park Theatre in New York with that role in November, 1825. It was during that run that Neagle painted the present portrait. Neagle later produced another depiction of Kean, an oil sketch in the character of Shylock (ca. 1855, The Pennsylvania Academy of the Arts).

References:
George C.D. Odell. *Annals of the New York Stage,* vol. III (1821-1834) New York: Columbia University Press, 1928, p. 134
[Mrs. John E. Owens.] *Memories of the Professional and Social Life of John E. Owens, by his Wife.* Baltimore: John Murphy and Co., 1892, p. 69
Pennsylvania Academy of the Fine Arts. *Catalogue of an Exhibition of Portraits by John Neagle,* essay by Mantle Fielding. Philadelphia: Pennsylvania Academy of the Fine Arts, 1925, pp. 11-13
The Players, *Catalogue of the Paintings and Art Treasures of The Players,* New York: The Players, 1925, p. 16, no. 81

1. Pennsylvania Academy of the Arts, *Catalogue of an Exhibition of Portraits by John Neagle,* essay by Mantle Fielding (Philadelphia: Pennsylvania Academy of the Fine Arts, 1925) p. 11. The commission was from Francis Courtney Wemyss, an actor-manager and Mr. Lopez, a prompter, for use in *The Acting American Theatre* published in 1826 by A. R. Poole.

2. *Catalogue of an Exhibition of Portraits by John Neagle,* p. 12. In the *Catalogue of the Paintings and Art Treasures of The Players* (New York: The Players, 1925) p. 16, the present portrait of Kean is referred to as the only one of the actor ever taken from life, and the beverage that inspired his cooperation is identified as champagne rather than brandy.

47
John Opie, R.A.
English, 1761-1807
Arthur Taken Prisoner, ca. 1786-1789
Oil on canvas, 72½ x 54½
The University of Virginia, Charlottesville, Virginia

King John's young nephew Arthur is a rival claimant to the English throne, supported by the French and many English nobles. In this scene Arthur is taken prisoner during a battle in France, and later, while still in John's custody, dies in a fall from a castle parapet. Opie has illustrated the line wherein John, here dressed in armor, instructs Hubert to "keep this boy."[1]

Opie was much influenced by the artistic theories of his older contemporary, Henry Fuseli. Unlike Fuseli, however, Opie never visited Italy and developed his style by absorbing the influences of English artists such as Fuseli, Reynolds and Benjamin West. *Arthur Taken Prisoner* reflects Opie's debt to Fuseli in the dramatic use of light and emphatic gesture and facial expression which convey the emotional tension of the moment. Like Fuseli, Opie was an important contributor to Boydell's Shakespeare Gallery.[2] This painting was executed for another, but similar scheme, the Irish Shakespeare Gallery initiated by James Woodmason in Dublin in 1792.[3] In 1806 Opie was elected Professor of Painting at the Royal Academy. His Academy lectures delivered in the following year were largely derived from Fuseli's ideas and served to disseminate them to the younger generation.

Exhibitions: Dublin: Irish Shakespeare Gallery, 1793; London: The New Shakespeare Gallery, 1794; London: Thomas Agnew and Sons, Ltd., *Three Centuries of British Painting*, 1978

References:
John J. Rogers, *Opie and His Works*, London: Colnaghi and Company, 1878, p. 195
Ada Earland, *John Opie and His Circle*, London: Hutchinson and Col, 1911, p. 335
Malcom C. Salaman, *Shakespeare in Pictorial Art*, London: The Studio, 1916, p. 25 illus.
Robin Hamlyn, "An Irish Shakespeare Gallery," *Burlington Magazine*, 120 (1978): pp. 515-29

---

1. The painting was also known as *The King Hubert and Arthur on the Battlefield* and *Scene from Shakespeare's play "King John."*

2. Opie painted five Shakespearean subjects for Boydell: *Leontes, Antigonius, Lords, Attendants and the Infant Perdita* from *The Winter's Tale*; *Countess, Porter, Talbot and c.* from *Henry VI, Part I*; *Mother Jourdain, Hume, Southwell, Bolingbrake and Eleanor* from *Henry VI, Part II*; *Timon, Alcibiades, Phrynia and Timandia* from *Timon of Athens* and *Friar Lawrence, Capulet, Lady Capulet, Paris, Friar, Nurse Musicians & c.* from *Romeo and Juliet*.

3. *Arthur Taken Prisoner* was exhibited in Dublin beginning May, 1793 with seventeen other Shakespearean subjects by artists such as Fuseli, William Hamilton, James Northcote and Matthew William Peters. The work was engraved by J. Fittler and published by Woodmason 1 August 1794. It was one of seventeen works included in *A Series of Engravings to Illustrate the Works of Shakespeare* published by John Murray in 1817 after the abandonment of the Irish Shakespeare Gallery scheme. At some time the canvas was altered by the addition of several inches of canvas to the top and bottom. See Robin Hamlyn "An Irish Shakespeare Gallery" *Burlington Magazine*, 120 (1978) pp. 520, 522 and 527.

4. Esther Gordon Dotson, "Shakespeare Illustration and Eugene Delacroix," *Essays in Honor of Walter Friedlander*, New York: Institute of Fine Arts, New York University, 1965, p. 47.

48
Matthew William Peters, R.A.
English, 1741-1814
Charmian and the Soothsayer
Oil on canvas, 60½ x 45¼
Mr. and Mrs. E. Hal Dickson, Mr. and Mrs. James R. Duncan and Mr. and Mrs. Frank W. Rose, San Angelo, Texas

Peters' *Charmian and the Soothsayer* was commissioned by James Woodmason in 1792 for the Irish Shakespeare Gallery, a project similar to Alderman Boydell's English scheme. Woodmason planned to produce an illustrated edition of the plays featuring engravings of the works in his Dublin gallery. Only twenty-three of the anticipated seventy-two works were completed, however, before the project was abandoned and the paintings sold. *Charmian* . . . was engraved by John Hall and published by John Murray in *A Series of Engravings to Illustrate the Works of Shakespeare*, 1817. The engraving shows a larger composition, suggesting that this work may have been cut down.[1]

In the scene depicted in the present work, a fortune-teller has been summoned by Alexas (the soldier in the background) to prophesy the future of Charmian by reading her palm. He foresees Charmian, who is a serving maid to Queen Cleopatra, outliving her mistress, a prediction which comes true when Charmian dies only moments after the Queen in the final act.

Following a period spent in France in the mid-1780s, Peters adopted the delicacy and elegance of French rococo painting. His manner of painting beautiful, and sensuous women, either luxuriantly dressed or suggestively undressed, made him one of the more popular contributors to Boydell's Shakespeare Gallery.[2] After 1778 he exhibited few paintings, preferring to devote his time to his second career as a clergyman in the Church of England.

Exhibitions: Dublin: Whistler's Great Room, Exchequer Street, *Irish Shakespeare Gallery*, 1793; London: Schomberg House, 88 Pall Mall, *The New Shakespeare Gallery*, 1794

References:

Robin Hamlyn, "An Irish Shakespeare Gallery," *Burlington Magazine*, 120 (1978): 515-529

Lady Victoria Manners, *Matthew William Peters, R.A.: His Life and Work*, London: The Connoisseur, 1913, pp. 51, 59, illus. pl. 7

Malcom Salaman, "Shakespeare in Pictorial Art" The Studio, 1916, p. 25, illus. p. 55

1. In his account of the Irish Shakespeare project, Robin Hamlyn indicates that the works were of a uniform size (66 x 54 inches) to facilitate engraving. The present work, which conforms to the engraving in other respects, is 5½ inches shorter and 8¾ narrower than this. See Robyn Hamlyn, "An Irish Shakespeare Gallery," *Burlington Magazine*, 120, 1978, p. 520. A painting of the same subject omitting the figure of Alexas, is reproduced in Victoria Manners, *Matthew William Peters, R.A., His Life and Work*, (London: The Connoisseur, 1913) plate 7.

2. Peters's works for the Boydell were *Mrs. Page with a Letter* from *Merry Wives of Windsor*, *Hero, Ursula and Beatrice* from *Much Ado About Nothing*; *The Queen and Her Women at Work*, *Cardinal Wolsey and Campeuis* from *King Henry VIII* and *The Christening of Queen Elizabeth* from *King Henry VIII*.

49
Matthew William Peters, R. A.
English, 1741-1814
The Merry Wives of Windsor (Falstaff in the Buck Basket)
Oil on canvas, 98 × 70
Museo-de Arte de Ponce, Fundacion Luis A. Ferre, Ponce, Puerto Rico

Peters contributed five works to the *Shakespeare Gallery* opened by Alderman John Boydell in 1789. Two of these works illustrate scenes from *The Merry Wives of Windsor* and are considered among the most accomplished of Peters' paintings. (The second, presently unlocated, is titled *Mrs. Ford and Mrs. Page Comparing Letters*.)

The present picture shows Mistresses Ford and Page secreting the old knight John Falstaff in a basket of dirty laundry. He is to be spirited out of Mrs. Ford's house by servants in time to avoid her suspicious husband who, the boy at the right informs them, is fast approaching. The scene is set before an open window with a view of Windsor Castle in the background. *Falstaff in the Buck Basket* was engraved for Boydell and published in 1793.[1]

Peters is known to have studied in Italy during the 1760s, but his charming feminine subjects in their splendid laces and fabrics appear more closely related to the styles of the French school.[2] *Falstaff in the Buck Basket* and the two other comedic paintings for Boydell were well received by the public, but Church authorities (Peters had taken holy orders in 1783) were less enthusiastic. Peters stated in a letter of 1790 that his clerical superiors had "expressed some displeasure" over his relationship with Boydell, owing most probably, to the paintings' boisterous and overtly sensual nature.

Reference:

Victoria Manners, *Matthew William Peters, R. A.: His Life and Work*, (London: The Connoisseiur, 1913) pp. 23, 55. illus. opp. p. 48

---

1. The work was engraved by Peter Simon and published 24 December 1793. A second printing is listed in the 1829 catalogue of Boys, Moon and Graves which indicates that both plain and colored versions were available. See Victoria Manners, *Matthew William Peters, R. A.: His Life and Works*, London: *The Connoisseur*, 1913, p. 62. The plate reproducing the engraving in Manners is tinted and may be derived from this colored version.

2. Peters' teacher Robert West had studied with Van Loo in Paris and may have inspired his pupil's Rococo mannerism, Manners, p. 2.

3. Manners, p. 24.

50   See Plate XV
Frederick Richard Pickersgill, R. A.
English, 1820-1900
Viola and the Countess, 1859
Oil on canvas, 36½ × 28¾
Signed with initials and dated lower center: FRP RA /
1859
Mr. and Mrs. E. Hal Dickson, Mr. and Mrs. James R. Duncan, and Mr. and Mrs. Frank W. Rose, San Angelo, Texas

This picture represents the scene in which Viola, disguised as a servant boy, has been sent by her master Orsino to press his suit for the hand of the Countess Olivia. Although she cruelly rejects Orsino, Olivia is enchanted by his servant who she mistakenly believes to be an eligible young gentleman. In Pickersgill's painting Olivia reveals her love to the perplexed Viola: "I love thee so that, maugre all thy pride,/ Nor wit nor reason can my passion hide."

The selfless devotion of Viola, who surpressed her own love for Orsino in helping him to pursue another, was greatly admired by the Victorians, and she was one of Shakespeare's most frequently depicted heroines.

Pickersgill's figures are highly idealized, and Viola is only thinly disguised in her embroidered tunic and red cape. Their eyes are large and expressive—Viola glances away in embarrassment at Olivia's pleading look of supplication—and there is a luxuriant sensuousness in the textures of flesh, hair and clothing. Although his flesh painting is solidly academic, reflecting the practice of his teacher William Etty, the strong linear quality and meticulous detail in Pickersgill's depiction of the costumes, the grass and the background elements reflect the strong influence of the Pre-Raphaelites upon other artists in the later 1850s.

51   See Plate XVI
Paul Falconer Poole
English, 1807-1879
A Scene from The Tempest, 1856
Oil on canvas, 35 × 38½
Signed and dated, lower right: P. F. Poole 1856
The FORBES Magazine Collection, New York

Paul Falconer Poole received no formal training as an artist, but was renowned in his own era as a superb colorist who imparted a "golden glow" to his finished works.[1] He participated in the 1840s project to decorate the newly constructed Houses of Parliament and, despite a scandalous personal life, was elected to the Royal Academy in 1861. The subjects of the paintings he exhibited at the Academy between 1830 and 1879 reveal his penchant for traditional literary subjects. His sources included the Bible, classical poetry and contemporary novels as well as Shakespeare's plays.

In this scene from *The Tempest*, the winged island spirit Ariel awakens the shipwrecked King of Naples just in time to prevent his murder by Sebastian and Antonio, the two knife-wielding figures at the left. The painting differs substantially from Shakespeare's text in showing King Alonso accompanied by three women and in depicting Ariel awakening him directly instead of by alerting his councillor Gonzalo, who here reclines undisturbed at the upper right. Despite these departures, the painting preserves the scene's result, i.e., the foiling of Sebastian and Antonio's murderous plot.

Poole's somewhat idiosyncratic methods of composition are well represented in this painting, where the contorted poses of the figures seem to meld into the configuration of the surrounding rocks.

---

1. Graham Reynolds, *Victorian Painting* (London: Studio Vista, 1966) pp. 142-143.

52
Paul Falconer Poole
English, 1807-1879
Triptych of studies for 'The Tempest'
Oil on canvas, 12 × 25
The FORBES Magazine Collection

In this small-scale oil study *A Scene from The Tempest* (cat. no. 51) serves as the central element in a triptych with two side panels.[1] The scheme is unified by the rock/cave structure running across the top of each section. The two flanking paintings both represent episodes involving Ferdinand and Miranda. At the left, the two lovers converse as Prospero looks on, and Caliban labors up the hill bearing a load of wood. At the right, Prospero and Alonso discover their children playing chess, an incident from Act V, scene i of the play.

1. The finished work was exhibited at the Royal Academy in 1849, nos. 383-385. The present locations of the two side panels are unknown.

53
Arthur Rackham
English, 1867-1939
'... Are you sure that we are awake ...', 1908
Ink and watercolor on illustration board, 11½ × 10⅜
Signed and dated lower right: Arthur Rackham.08
Folger Shakespeare Library, Washington, D.C.

The play A *Midsummer Night's Dream* with elements of fantasy and English folklore was ideally suited to the talents of Arthur Rackham, whose fairytale illustrations are universally beloved. 'Are you sure that we are awake' was one of a series of illustrations for A *Midsummer Night's Dream* executed for a 1908 edition of the play published by William Heinemann.[1]

The illustration depicts the four lovers—Demetrius, Helena, Hermia and Lysander—wandering the forest in bewilderment after an evening spent under the spell of the Fairy King, Oberon.[2] Their faces express surprise at the forest's changed aspect—the enchantment of the previous night is past and the twisting branches seem threatening in the light of day. As a draughtsman of exceptional talent, Rackham had a special sensitivity to the qualities of objects such as trees. His calligraphic line provides them with a separate identity equal to, or often more important, than that of the humans in his work.

Rackham trained only part-time as an artist in an evening course at the Lambeth School of Art, London. The process of photoengraving, which revolutionized illustration in the 1890s by adding heightened color capability, was instrumental in Rackham's success as an illustrator for books and periodicals, such as *The Graphic* and *Punch*. A second Shakespearean favorite was *The Tempest*, a version of which was published by Heinemann's in 1926.

Exhibition: London: Leicester Galleries, 1908

Reference:

"A Midsummer Night's Dream" London and New York: William Heinemann and Charles Scribner's Sons, 1908. illus. opposite page 102 in English edition

---

1. Rackham illustrated four versions of A *Midsummer Night's Dream*. The 1908 edition was reissued in 1913 with colors added to the original line drawings. In addition, he executed a special series of drawings for the New York Public Library's Spencer Collection in 1929, two editions of Charles and Mary Lamb's *Tales from Shakespeare* in 1899 and 1909 and a Limited Editions Club version in 1939. Roland Baughman, *The Centenary of Arthur Rackham's Birth* (New York: Columbia University Libraries, 1967) p. 13.

2. The Berol Collection at Columbia University owns three of Rackham's sketchbooks related to illustrations for A *Midsummer Night's Dream*. Baughman, p. 45.

54
Joshua Reynolds, P. R. A.
English, 1723-1792
A Study for King Lear
Oil on canvas, 29½ x 24½
Mrs. E. Hal Dickson, Mr. and Mrs. James R. Duncan and
Mr. and Mrs. Frank W. Rose, San Angelo, Texas

Joshua Reynolds was the first president of the Royal Academy and the major proponent of English history painting in the grand manner associated with Continental schools of art. His *Discourses*, delivered as lectures to students at the Royal Academy between 1769 and 1790, defined the aesthetic outlook of the eighteenth century as a rational, academic doctrine and influenced English painting into the nineteenth century. John Boydell considered Reynolds' participation in his *Shakespeare Gallery* necessary to its success and, commissioned three works from him.[1]

Reynolds painted a head of Lear, which was a part of his personal collection in 1773, and was engraved at least twice.[2] The surviving engravings document the appearance of this work. It is last known to have been shown at the British Institution in 1813 as a part of the collection of Lady Thomond, identified as a portrait of Charles Macklin in the role of Lear.[3]

1. Reynolds was given £500 by Boydell in advance of the three pictures he commissioned for the Gallery. The three were *Puck* (or *Robin Goodfellow*) (ca. 1799, Earl Fitzwilliam, Milton Park, Peterborough) *Macbeth Visiting the Witches* (Petworth) and the most celebrated of the collection's works, *Death of Cardinal Beaufort* (Petworth). Winifred H. Friedman, *Boydell's Shakespeare Gallery* (New York: Garland Publishing Inc., 1976) 112.

2. In James Northcote's memoirs of Reynolds, he recounts the visit of a young painter of miniatures, Ozias Humphrey, who copied a head of Lear by Sir Joshua which was in the older artist's personal collection. James Northcote, *The Life of Joshua Reynolds*, Vol. II (London: Henry Colburn, Conduit Street, 1819) 176-77. The engravings which correspond to the composition are a mezzotint, 12¼ x 9⅞, possibly by Marchi and a line engraving by W. Sharp, 6⅜ x 5½, published 1 May 1783 by John Boydell. Edward Hamilton, *The Engraved Works of Sir Joshua Reynolds*, London, 1884 (reprint Amsterdam, 1973) 151.

3. Algernon Graves, *A Century of Loan Exhibitions 1813-1912*, vol II, (London: Kings Meads Reprints).

55
George Romney
English, 1734-1802
Macbeth's Meeting With the Witches, ca. 1780
Oil on canvas, 29½ x 24¹⁵⁄₁₆
Folger Shakespeare Library, Washington, D.C.

This painting is said to represent the actor John Henderson in the role of Macbeth, in the scene in which he goes to the witches' cave and is shown prophetic and ghostly apparitions, including the procession of kings that appears in the background. The horrific faces of the witches and Macbeth's dramatic lunge display the intensity of expression recommended in Fuseli's prescriptions for "epic" or "dramatic" painting. The painting relates in subject and composition to *John Henderson as Macbeth*, a largely destroyed work by Romney, showing the actor in three-quarter length, holding a cap in his right hand and a sword in his left.[1] As in the present work, the witches were placed at the right and a procession of kings was seen in the background. There are several other sketches by Romney of Henderson in the role showing variations in the figure.[2]

Henderson was one of the most prominent actors of Romney's day. He and the painter moved in the same circles of literati, actors and artists, and were fellow members of the Unincreasable Club.

Exhibition: Washington, D.C.: Federal Reserve Board, *According to Shakespeare: 18th and 19th Century English Painting*, 1976-77 (no. 19)

Reference:

Patricia Jaffé: *Drawings by George Romney*, Cambridge: Fitzwilliam Museum, 1977, p. 26

1. Humprey Ward and William Roberts, *Romney: A Biographical and Critical Essay with A Catalogue Raisonné of his Works*, vol. II, (London: Thomas Agnew and Sons, 1904) p. 76. The first version of this work is believed to have been cut down from its original size (54½ x 64½") to 50 x 40", to leave only the figure of Henderson. Jennifer Watson, *George Romney in Canada* (Ontario: Kitchner/Waterloo Art Gallery, 1985) 61-62. A replica of this work (35 x 28") as it originally existed is found in the collection of the Garrick Club. It was engraved in mezzotint by John Jones, 19 May, 1787.
2. Patricia Jaffé, *Drawings by George Romney* (Cambridge: Fitzwilliam Museum, 1977) 24-27, nos. 40 and 41.

56
George Romney
English, 1734-1802
The Infant Shakespeare Attended by Nature and the Passions, ca. 1789-1793
Oil on canvas, 56 × 80
Folger Shakespeare Library, Washington, D.C.

George Romney was, with Sir Joshua Reynolds and Thomas Gainsborough, one of the most highly regarded English portraitists of the eighteenth century. Like many of his contemporaries, however, Romney aspired to paint great subject pictures and considered Shakespeare an important source for such themes.

The Infant Shakespeare Attended by Nature and the Passions was painted for Boydell's Shakespeare Gallery and published in 1803. Unlike the other Boydell pictures it does not illustrate an episode from the plays. It is described in the Boydell catalogue of 1793: "Nature is represented with her face unveiled to her favourite child, who is placed between Joy and Sorrow. On the right hand of Nature are Love, Hatred and Jealousy; on her left hand, Anger, Envy and Fear."[1]

Garrick's Shakespeare Jubilee of 1769 officially elevated the playwright into the pantheon of English history. By placing Shakespeare in supernatural company, Romney certifies his genius as timeless and implies that his greatness was preordained from birth. Other artists, notably Joshua Reynolds, made use of similar enobling devices.[2] The personifications of the Passions reveal Romney's knowledge of compositions by Henry Fuseli and accord with Fuseli's belief that "what is painted stands for and evokes our recognition above and beyond the visible." Their emblematic, mask-like visages were intended to represent the universal concept of each emotion. The faces of Love and Joy are said to have been derived from a specific source—drawings of Emma Hart (later Lady Hamilton), Romney's favorite model. Emma is also featured in a related allegorical work painted by Romney for Boydell, *Shakespeare Nursed by Comedy and Tragedy.*[3]

Exhibitions: London: The Boydell Shakespeare Gallery; London: The Royal Institute, 1848, 1863; London: The Grafton Gallery, 1900; Washington, D.C.: Folger Shakespeare Library, *Shakespeare: The Globe and the World,* 1979; Washington, D.C.: Federal Reserve Board, *According to Shakespeare: 18th 19th Century English Painting,* 1976-1977, (no. 8)

References:

Humphrey Ward and William Roberts. *Romney: A Biographical and Critical Essay with a Catalogue Raisonne of his Works.* New York: Charles Scribners' Sons, 1904, p. 194

Winifred Friedman. *Boydell's Shakespeare Gallery.* New York: Garland Publishing Inc., 1976, pp. 128-138, illus.

Yvonne Dixon. *Catalogue Raisonne of the Drawings of George Romney in the Folger Shakespeare Library.* (PhD Dissertation, University of Maryland, 1977), pp. 314-316

Samuel Schoenbaum. *Shakespeare, The Globe and the World.* New York: Folger Shakespeare Library and Oxford University Press, 1979, p. 186, illus.

1. Quoted in Yvonne Dixon. *Catalogue Raisonne of the Drawings of George Romney in the Folger Shakespeare Library* (PhD Dissertation, University of Maryland, 1977) p. 314, states that the painting was inspired by an earlier work, destroyed in the artist's lifetime, titled *Nature Unveiling Herself to Shakespeare* which was, in turn, based on Thomas Gray's "The Progress of Posey." Dixon believes that Romney's inclusion of the Passions was inspired by William Collins' poem "Ode on the Passions." *The Infant Shakespeare...* was engraved by Benjamin Smith for Boydell. An oil sketch for the painting is in the collection of the Royal Shakespeare Theatre at Stratford-on-Avon. See Humphrey Ward and W. Roberts, *Romney: A Biographical and Critical Essay with a Catalogue Raisonne of his Works,* Vol. II, (New York: Charles Scribner's Sons, 1904) p. 193.

2. In Winifred H. Friedman, *Boydell's Shakespeare Gallery* (New York: Garland Publishing, Inc. 1976) p. 136, Friedman Reynold's *Garrick Between Tragedy and Comedy.* Reynolds's *Mrs. Siddons as the Tragic Muse* is conceived in a similar vein.

3. Romney sketched Lady Hamilton for two other Boydell paintings, notably as Miranda for *The Enchanted Island: Before the Call of Prospero,* Volume One and *Cassandra Raving,* both published by Boydell. The masks of the Passions have been identified with the actresses Siddons and Kemble (see letter from Cockerell to Wells dated 15 July 1927 in the files of the Folger Library), and a number of sketches are identified as studies (see Friedman, p. 137 and Folger Art Volumes 60. 101-103 and Art Flat 67, 70, 72).

57
Dante Gabriel Rossetti
English, 1828-1882
The Death of Lady Macbeth, ca. 1875
Pencil on paper, 18¾ × 24½
Inscribed, lower left: The Death of Lady Macbeth/DGR/ 1876
[?partially erased]
Carlisle Museum and Art Gallery, Carlisle, England

Dante Gabriel Rossetti produced some of the nineteenth century's most distinctive, romantic images of women and, with William Holman Hunt and John Everett Millais, was a founder of the highly influential Pre-Raphaelite Brotherhood. After the untimely death of his wife Elizabeth Siddal in 1862, Rossetti's work became increasingly moody, pervaded by an obsession with death and spirituality.

In Act V, scene i, Lady Macbeth approaches death surrounded by a physician and attendants who close around her crouching, tormented body. Her anguished gestures and the scene's morbid atmosphere reveal the influence of works by Henry Fuseli and Theodore von Holst, two artists Rossetti admired.[1] Rossetti's model for Lady Macbeth was Jane Morris, the friend and model frequently depicted in his late work. The drawing is dated on the basis of style to around 1875, and demonstrates the artist's technical facility.[2]

Rossetti typically chose literary themes rather than the landscapes, religious, or modern life subjects favored by the other Pre-Raphaelites. In addition to scenes from medieval literature, he depicted Shakespearean characters such as *Mariana* (1868-70, Aberdeen Art Gallery) and *Hamlet and Ophelia* (ca. 1854-59, British Museum).

Exhibitions: Newcastle-upon-Tyne: Laing Art Gallery, *The Pre-Raphaelites*, 1974; London: The Royal Academy, *Rossetti: Poet and Painter*, 1973; Buxton: Buxton Museum and Art Gallery, *Shakespeare's Heroines in the Nineteenth Century*, 1980 (no. 30); London: The Tate Gallery, *The Pre-Raphaelites*, 1984 (no. 294)

References:

Virginia Surtees, *The Paintings and Drawings of Dante Gabriel Rossetti (1828-1882)*. Oxford: The Clarendon Press, 1974, p. 140, no. 242, illus. pl. 352
Geoffrey Ashton. *Shakespeare's Heroines in the Nineteenth Century*. Buxton: Museum and Art Gallery, 1980, p. 64, no. 30, illus.
The Tate Gallery. *The Pre-Raphaelites*. London: The Tate Gallery, 1984, p. 308, no. 249. illus.

1. The Tate Gallery, *The Pre-Raphaelites* (London: The Tate Gallery/Penguin Books, 1984) p. 308.

2. Virginia Surtees, *The Paintings and Drawings of Dante Gabriel Rossetti 1828-1882* (Oxford: Clarendon Press, 1971) 140. The Carlisle version (cat. 242) is the most finished version of the subject. Nos. 242 A, B and C are study drawings for this work.

58
James Sant, R.A.
English, 1820-1916
Ophelia
Oil on canvas, 30 × 25
Signed in monogram lower right: JS
Mr. and Mrs. E. Hal Dickson, Mr. and Mrs. James R. Duncan and Mr. and Mrs. Frank W. Rose, San Angelo, Texas

The litany of herbs and flowers recited by Ophelia in her mad distraction provided artists with recognizable attributes for this gentle, pathetic character. In Sant's portrait, these flowers provide the key to the identification of the figure, which otherwise conforms to the common Victorian type of innocent girlhood.

Sant's visualization of Ophelia resembles the type popularized in the idealized engravings of female figures found in Books of Beauty or Keepsake volumes.[1] In this case, the model is a child (Sant was especially known as a painter of children) who appears startled rather than insane. Ophelia's long flowing hair and delicate drapery echo the delicacy of the flowers in this appealing image. Sant was much in demand for works in this vein during his long career. He was elected to the Royal Academy in 1869 and in 1878 was appointed Principal Painter in Ordinary to Queen Victoria.

Reference:
The Studio, 68, (1916) p. 176

---

1. Geoffrey Ashton, *Shakespeare's Heroines in the Nineteenth Century* (Buxton: Museum and Art Gallery, 1980), p. iv.

59 See Plate XVII
Robert Smirke
English, 1752-1845
Falstaff Examining Prince Hal
Oil on canvas, 62½ × 86⅜
Bob Jones University, Greenville, South Carolina

Robert Smirke was one of the earliest and most influential interpreters of Shakespeare, primarily through his contributions to illustrated editions of the plays derived from the native artistic traditions of Hogarth and Hayman that appeared from the 1780s to the 1820s.[1] His many and varied compositions preserve the basic English qualities of the characters.[2]

Falstaff was a favorite source of merriment and humor both on the stage and in art; he figures in three of Shakespeare's most popular plays. His character was gradually codified into that of a paunchy Elizabethan-costumed soldier of dubious repute. *King Henry IV, Part I* is the source for this version of a Boydell Shakespeare Gallery painting which illustrates Falstaff playing the role of Hal's father the King. "This chair shall be my state, this dagger my sceptre, and this cushion my crown," he says as he begins questioning Hal about his dissolute life and questionable companions. His buffoonish appearance is contrasted with the sober portrait of the King on the wall behind Hal's head.

Smirke supplied 26 paintings to the Boydell project, more than any other artist. This work shows some variation from the corresponding Boydell engraving by Robert Thew. In the present painting, the drapery and figure at the back left have been sketched in and a feather added to the figure's hat. The position of Falstaff's left arm has been adjusted and further foreshortened. Some details of costume (the Prince's garters for example) are simplified or omitted. Smirke's work for Boydell evidently took the form of "finished sketches" in some cases, a situation which may explain some of the differences between this painting and the engraving.[3]

---

1. Smirke and Thomas Stothard produced a volume of thirty-two illustrations for *The Picturesque Beauties of Shakespeare, being A Selection of Scenes, from the Works of that Great Author*. London, 1783-87. He contributed illustrations to *The Plays of Shakespeare*, London: Longman, Hurst, Rees, and Orme, 1807; Elizabeth Inchbald, *The British Theatre*, London: Longman, Hurst, Rees and Orme, 1808. *Illustrations to Shakespeare by Robert Smirke, R.A.*, London: Rodwell and Martin, 1821-22 and *Illustrations to Shakespeare by Robert Smirke, R.A.*, London: Hurst, Robinson and Company and R. Jennings, 1825. See Esther Gordon Dotson's "English Shakespeare Illustration and Eugene Delacroix" in *Essays in Honor of Walter Friedlaender*, New York: Institute of Fine Arts, New York University, 1965, p. 45, details Delacroix's use of Smirke's illustrations in the development of his own Shakespearean subjects.

2. T. S. R. Boase, "Illustrations of Shakespeare's Plays in the Seventeenth and Eighteenth Centuries," *Journal of the Warburg and Courtauld Institutes*, 10 (1947) pp. 96, 100.

3. Winifred Friedman, *Boydell's Shakespeare Gallery*, New York and London: Garland Publishing Inc. 1976, p. 202. Friedman cites an excerpt from the *Farington Diary*, July 3, 1794, vol. I, p. 189.

60 See Plate XVIII
Thomas Sully
American, 1783-1872
George Frederick Cooke as Richard III, 1811
Oil on canvas, 95 x 60½
Signed and dated (lower right):   TS 1811
The Pennsylvania Academy of Fine Arts, Philadelphia,
presented by Friends and Admirers of the Artist

The highlight of the Philadelphia theatrical season in 1811 was the performance of George Frederick Cooke, an English actor renowned for his interpretations of Shakespearean roles. His mercurial temperament and drinking habits were the bane of theatrical managers' existence, but did not detract from his immense popularity. Thomas Sully left this account of his famous sitter: "He was a *bon-vivant* and a wonderful actor. When I saw him act in Philadelphia it was very difficult to get into the house."[1]

Sully began painting this portrait and two others of Cooke about two weeks after the actor's arrival in Philadelphia in April of 1811.[2] Cooke is shown wearing his own costume, standing before a stage setting with niche and sculpted figure. The actor presents the villainous usurper and murderer as a powerful man with a hooded gaze of cunning deceit, in contrast to the sweet and gentle countenance of the statue behind him. The low viewpoint, which lends the actor heroic stature, and the expert command of textures in the costume and setting reflect Sully's study with Sir Thomas Lawrence during his visit to London in 1809-1810. The work was said to reproduce so faithfully the likeness and presence of the actor (the correlation between Cooke's personality and that of the role was apparently not unremarked) that it was placed on the stage for a memorial service after his death in New York in 1812.

Sully became acquainted with theatrical subjects early in life. His parents were both actors and emigrated from England to Charleston, South Carolina in 1792. One of Sully's earliest portraits was of the English actor Thomas Abthorpe Cooper, who pursuaded him to visit New York and secured many commissions for the young portraitist.

Exhibitions: Washington, D.C.: The National Portrait Gallery, *Portraits of the American Stage*, 1971 (no. 4); Cincinnati: Cincinnati Art Museum, *Exhibition of Pennsylvania Academy of the Fine Arts Paintings*, 1974; London: The United States Christopher M.S. Johns, "Theatre and Theory: Thomas Sully's *George Frederick Cooke as Richard III*," *Winterthur Portfolio* 18 (1983) pp. 27-38, illus. Embassy, *Young America*, 1975; Glasgow: Glasgow Art Gallery and Museum, 1975; Bristol: City Art Gallery, 1975; New York: Whitney Museum of American Art, 1976; Stratford, Ontario: The Gallery/Stratford, *Fantastic Shakespeare*, 1978 (no. 57); Los Angeles: Los Angeles County Museum of Art and the National Portrait Gallery, *American Portraiture in the Grand Manner, 1720-1920*, 1982; Washington, D.C.: The National Portrait Gallery, *Thomas Sully*, 1983

References:

Sadakichi Hartmann, *Shakespeare in Art*, Boston: L. D. Paget, 1900, p. 339, 341 illus. p. 339

Edward Biddle and Mantle Fielding. *The Life and Works of Thomas Sully 1783-1872*, Philadelphia: Wickersham Press, 1921, p. 23, p. 127

W. Moelwyn Merchant, *Shakespeare and the Artist*, London: Oxford University Press, 1959, p. 115

Los Angeles County Museum, *American Portraiture in the Grand Manner, 1720-1920*. Essays by Michael Quick, Marvin Sadik and William Gerdts, Catalogue by Michael Quick. Los Angeles: Los Angeles County Museum of Art, 1981, p. 129, illus. pl. 28

Monroe Fabian. *Mr. Sully; Portrait Painter: The Works of Thomas Sully (1783-1872)*. Washington: The National Portrait Gallery, 1983, p. 56, illus. pl. 17

1. Quoted in Edward Biddle and Mantle Fielding, *The Life and Works of Thomas Sully (1783-1872)* Philadelphia: Wickersham Press, 1921, p. 23.

2. Biddle and Fielding list a total of five portraits of Cooke in their catalogue of his works, nos. 366-370. No. 370 probably corresponds to a copy of Sully's portrait made for Edwin Forrest in 1817 and now in the collection of the Garrick Club, London. William Dunlap in his *Life of Cooke*, discusses Sully's portraits in volume two, p. 256. See William Dunlap, *The Life of Cooke* (2nd edition) two volumes, London: Printed for Henry Colburn . . . 1815, p. 256.

3. Biddle and Fielding p. 23, taken from the "Recollections" of William B. Wood. W. Moelwyn Merchant, *Shakespeare and the Artist* note I, p. 115, notes the recurring use of niches and sculptures in backgrounds in theatrical pictures. See Daniel Maclise's *Play Scene from 'Hamlet'*, no. 40.

61   See Plate XIX
Thomas Sully
American, 1783-1872
Portia and Shylock, 1835
Oil on canvas, 38 x 29
Signed and dated (lower right):   T.S. 1835
The Folger Shakespeare Library, Washington, D.C.

Some forty years after painting Cooke as Richard III, Sully was commissioned to illustrate this scene for Edward Carey, a Philadelphia patron and President of the Pennsylvania Academy of Fine Arts.[1]

An inscription formerly visible upon the reverse of the painting indicates that it depicts Act IV, scene i, lines 230-232.[2] Portia holds the bond within her fingers as if to tear it, but Shylock gestures to prevent this, brandishing the scales with which he insists he will measure his pound of Antonio's flesh.

All attention is focused on the lovely and clever Portia—Shylock and the two minor figures in the background are more summarily painted and cast in shadow. The light illuminating Portia's face reveals the delicate, classic beauty with which Sully graced his female sitters. The pose of her head and neck recall Sully's many portraits of English actress Fanny Kemble, several also painted in the 1830s, in Shakespearean roles.[3]

Reference:
Edward Biddle and Mantle Fielding, *The Life and Works of Thomas Sully (1783-1872)* Philadelphia: Wikersham Press, 1921, p. 379, no. 2514

---

1. Carey apparently commissioned a series of portraits of Shakespearean heroines from Sully. The others include *Isabella* (Biddle and Fielding 2346), *Juliet* (2357), and *Lady Macbeth* (2405), both painted between 1836 and 1840. During the same period (1835-36) he also painted *Miranda* (2421). Gabriel Wells has suggested that *Portia and Shylock* may have been engraved by J. B. Forrest for illustration in a book. This information was provided by Katherine Johnson of the Folger.

2. The inscription copied during previous restoration reads: "Portia Be merciful. Take thrice thy money. Bid me tear the bond. Shylock, when it is paid according to the tenour. Vide Merchant of Venice Act IV, scene i ?? 1835."

3. The Kemble family members were intimates of Thomas Lawrence, with whom Sully studied in London, and they formed a close friendship with Sully during a visit to America in 1832. Biddle and Fielding list thirteen portraits of Fanny Kemble (catalogue numbers 949-961). No. 950 in the character of Juliet, 951 and 52 in that of Bianca, 954 as Lady Macbeth, 955 as Beatrice. The Portia of this painting does not resemble Kemble, who was dark haired and had a fuller face.

62
Edward Matthew Ward
English, 1816-1879
King Lear and Cordelia, 1857
Oil on canvas, 53 × 62
Mr. and Mrs. E. Hal Dickson, Mr. and Mrs. James R. Duncan and Mr. and Mrs. Frank R. Rose, San Angelo, Texas

In the scene here depicted, King Lear has been rescued from his harrowing night on the moors and awakens to discover his daughter Cordelia at his side. His startled expression reflects the disquiet of his mind—"You are a spirit . . ." he tells Cordelia. As the physician and attendants surround them, Cordelia laments her father's distressed condition—"Was this a face to be opposed against the warring winds? To stand against the deep dread-bolted thunder?"

Ward incorporates a profusion of theatrical details into the scene, and the hanging drapery gives it a stage-like aspect. The musicians outside provide the music called for in the stage directions, although the scene is placed in a cave rather than Shakespeare's tent. Other elements are unabashedly exotic, such as the tiger skins on the King's couch, the golden ewer and goblet on the table, and Cordelia's bejeweled and brocaded cape. The whole is visualized in a sumptous manner that reflects the theatrical staging of the period. Ward mastered his polished academic technique during his training in Rome, from 1836-1839, and in Munich, where he studied with the Nazarene Peter van Cornelius. His experience with the muralist Cornelius may have been a significant factor in the decision to award him commissions for three frescoes in the New Houses of Parliament in 1853.

63
Benjamin West
English (born America) 1738-1820
Romeo and Juliet, 1778
Oil on canvas, 50 × 44¼
Signed and dated lower right: B. West. London/ 1778
New Orleans Museum of Art

Born an innkeeper's son in Lancaster, Pennsylvania, Benjamin West went on to become one of the key figures in later eighteenth-century English painting. Leaving America in 1759, he studied art in Rome for three years before settling in London to pursue a career as a history painter. West rapidly gained the respect of his contemporaries and was a founding member of the Royal Academy in England. In 1770 his painting *Death of General Wolfe* (National Gallery of Canada, Ottawa) redefined history painting in contemporary terms, establishing a new genre. He was an influential teacher and mentor of younger artists, especially fellow Americans who flocked to his studio. His distinguished career was punctuated with two exceptional honors: his appointment as history painter to King George III and, in 1792, election to the presidency of the Royal Academy. West preferred subjects taken from classical literature and the Bible, but also depicted a number of Shakespearean scenes. He was an important contributor to Boydell's Shakespeare Gallery.[1]

In *Romeo and Juliet* West depicts Romeo's hasty departure following his secret marriage to Juliet. Juliet's nurse rushes into her chamber to warn of the impending arrival of her mother Lady Capulet, as Romeo hurries to avoid detection. The graceful figures and the background landscape show the influence of the Italian Neo-Classicist Raphael Mengs, absorbed by West during his years in Rome. The agitated expression of the nurse and her lunging pose may reflect the influence of West's contemporary Henry Fuseli. The painting was purchased in 1779 by the Duke of Courland, who also purchased a *Lear and Cordelia* from the artist.[2]

Exhibition: Ontario: The Gallery/Stratford, *Fantastic Shakespeare*, 1978 (no. 60)

References:

The Gallery/Stratford. Fantastic Shakespeare Ontario: The Gallery/Stratford, 1978, illus., no. 60

New Orleans Museum of Art. *Handbook of the Collection*, 1980, p. 127, illus.

Lovers, ed. Mary Laurence. New York: Balance House Ltd. and A&W Publishers, Inc., 1982, illus.

---

1. West's two paintings for the Boydell Shakespeare Gallery were *Lear, Kent, Fool, Edgar disguised as a Madman, and Gloster with a Torch* from *King Lear* and *King, Queen, Laertes, Ophelia and ect.* from *Hamlet*.
2. The work was engraved twice. The first engraving, by G. Scorodonow, dated 1775, is a detail of the figures of Romeo and Juliet. The second is a line engraving in reverse, made by William Sharp in 1783. This information was generously provided by Professor Allen Staley from his forthcoming catalogue raisonné of West's paintings.

64
Johann Zoffany
English, (born Germany) 1734/5-1810
Charles Macklin as Shylock, c. 1768
Oil on canvas, 32 x 28
National Theatre of Great Britain, London

Shakespeare's Shylock is one of the dramatist's most intriguing characters, simultaneously evoking emotions of sympathy and revulsion in his audience. Zoffany's portrait of Charles Macklin shows the actor's impassioned performance as he demands justice—his "pound of flesh"—in a Venetian courtroom.[1]

Macklin's performance of the role of Shylock was a milestone in the history of British theatre. In place of the customary low comedy, he introduced a new tragic interpretation, adopting the characteristics and dress of contemporary Jews in developing the part.[2] He preceded Garrick in abandoning the declamatory style of acting for a more natural delivery. He first played Shylock in 1741, but this painting is probably based on performances at Covent Garden in the 1767-68 season.[3]

Johann Zoffany's ties with the theatre were first established through his friendship with the actor David Garrick, who figures in many of his theatrical conversation pieces. These follow Hogarth in showing groups of actors as they appeared in productions at the time. Zoffany was especially admired for his skill in reproducing likenesses, details of setting and costume, and the impact of individual performances.

Exhibition: London: Hayward Gallery, The Georgian Playhouse: *Actors, Artists, Audiences and Architecture*, 1730-1830, 1975, no. 31

References:
The Arts Council of Great Britain. *The Georgian Playhouse: Actors, Artists, Audiences and Architecture 1730-1830* London: Arts Council of Great Britain, 1975, no. 31

1. There are many engravings of Macklin in the role of Shylock and several paintings attributed to Zoffany, including a preparatory study of head and shoulders in the National Gallery of Ireland which relates to the National Theatre's portrait. See Arts Council of Great Britain. *The Georgian Playhouse: Actors, Artists and Architecture, 1730-1830.* (London: The Arts Council of Great Britain, 1975) n.p. no. 31.

2. Esther Gordon Dotson. *Shakespeare Illustrated* (PhD Dissertation, New York University, 1973) p. 18.

3. *The Georgian Playhouse* . . . no. 31.

BIBLIOGRAPHY

Adams, C. K. *A Catalogue of the Pictures in the Garrick Club*. London: The Garrick Club, 1935.

Altick, Richard D. *The Shows of London: A Panoramic History of Exhibitions 1600-1862*. Cambridge: Harvard University Press, 1978.

The Arts Council of Great Britain. *The Georgian Playhouse: Actors, Artists Audiences and Architecture, 1730-1830*. Catalogue by Iain Mackintosh and Geoffrey Ashton. London: The Arts Council, 1976.

_____. *Shakespeare in Art*. Essay by William Moelwyn Merchant, Catalogue by Ronald Pickvance. London: The Arts Council, 1964.

Ashton, Geoffrey. *Shakespeare and British Art*. New Haven: Yale Center for British Art, 1981.

_____. *Shakespeare's Heroines in the Nineteenth Century*. Buxton: Museum and Art Gallery, 1980.

Bartholomeusz, Dennis. *The Winter's Tale in Performance in England and America, 1611-1976*. Cambridge: Cambridge University Press, 1982.

Berry, Ralph. "Beerbohm Tree as Director: Three Shakespeare Productions." *Essays in Theatre* 1 (1883): 73-80.

Bertelsen, Lance. "David Garrick and English Painting." *Eighteenth Century Studies*. 11 (1978): 308-24.

Boase, Thomas Sherer Ross. "The Decoration of the New Palace of Westminister." *Journal of the Warburg and Courtauld Institutes* 17 (1954):

_____. "Illustrations of Shakespeare's Plays in the Seventeenth and Eighteenth Centuries." *The Journal of the Warburg and Courtauld Institutes*. 10 (1947): 83-108.

Booth, Michael R. *Victorian Spectacular Theatre, 1850-1910*. Boston: Routledge and Kegan Paul, 1981.

Borowitz, Helen O. " 'King Lear' in the Art of Ford Madox Brown." *Victorian Studies* 21 (1978): 309-34.

Boydell, John. *The Boydell Shakespeare Prints*. Introduction by A. E. Santaniello. New York: B. Blom, 1968.

David and Alfred Smart Gallery. *Alderman Boydell's Shakespeare Gallery*. Introduction by Richard W. Hutton, catalogue by Laura Nelke. Chicago: Smart Gallery, 1978.

Dotson, Esther Gordon. "Shakespeare Illustrated, 1770-1820." PhD dissertation, New York University, 1973.

_____. "English Shakespeare Illustration and Eugene Delacroix." *Essays in Honor of Walter Friedlander*. New York: Institute of Fine Arts, New York University, 1965, pp. 40-61.

Erffa, Helmut von. "King Lear by Benjamin West." *Rhode Island School of Design Bulletin*. 43 (1956): 6-7.

Forbes, Christopher. *The Royal Academy Revisited 1837-1901*. New York: The Forbes Collection, 1975.

Foulkes, Richard. "Herbert Beerbohm Tree's Henry VIII: Expenditure, Spectacle and Experiment." *Theatre Research International* 3 (1977): 22-32.

Friedman, Winifred. *Boydell's Shakespeare Gallery*. New York: Garland, 1976.

The Gallery/Stratford. *Fantastic Shakespeare*, Stratford, Ontario: The Gallery/Stratford, 1978.

Guildhall Art Gallery. *Shakespeare and the Theatre*. Catalogue by Sybil Rosenfeld. London: Guildhall Art Gallery, 1964.

Hamlyn, Robin. "An Irish Shakespeare Gallery." *Burlington Magazine* 120 (1978): 515-29.

Hartmann, Sadakichi: *Shakespeare in Art*. Boston: L. C. Paget, 1900.

Hughes, Alan. *Henry Irving, Shakespearean*. Cambridge: Cambridge University Press, 1981.

Kerslake, John F. *Catalogue of Theatrical Portraits in London Public Collections*. London: Society for Theatre Research, 1961.

Mander, Raymond and Joe Mitchenson. *The Artist and the Theatre*. London: William Heinemann, Ltd., 1955.

_____. *Guide to the Maugham Collection of Theatrical Paintings*. London: National Theatre and William Heinemann, 1980.

Mazer, Cary. *Shakespeare Refashioned: Elizabethan Plays on Edwardian Stages*. Ann Arbor: U.M.I. Research Press, 1981.

Merchant, William Moelwyn. "Francis Hayman's Illustrations of Shakespeare." *Shakespeare Quarterly* 9 (1958): 385-87.

_____. "John Runciman's 'Lear in the Storm'." *Journal of the Warburg and Courtauld Institutes* 17 (1954): 385-87.

_____. *Shakespeare and the Artist*. London: Oxford University Press, 1959.

Meisel, Martin. *Realizations: Narrative, Pictorial and Dramatic Arts in Nineteenth Century England*. Princeton: Princeton University Press, 1983.

Mullin, Michael. "Strange Images of Death: Sir Herbert Beerbohm Tree's Macbeth." *Theatre Survey* 17 (1976): 125-142.

Oakley, Lucy. "The Evolution of Sir John Everett Millais's *Portia*." *Metropolitan Museum Journal* 16 (1981): 181-94.

The Players. *Catalogue of the Paintings and Art Treasures of The Players*. New York: The Players, 1925.

Paulson, Ronald. *Book and Painting: Shakespeare, Milton, and the Bible: Literary Texts and the Emergence of English Painting* (The Hodges Lectures). Knoxville: University of Tennessee Press, 1982.

Poulson, Christine. "A Checklist of Pre-Raphaelite Illustrations of Shakespeare's Plays." *Burlington Magazine* 122 (1980): 244-50.

Ripley, John. "'Imagination Holds Dominion: Stage Spectacles in Beerbohm Tree's Productions, 1897-1900." *Theatre Survey* 9 (1969): 11-20.

Rosenfeld, Sybil. *A Short History of Scene Design in Great Britain*. Oxford: Basil Blackwell, 1973.

Rowell, George. *Theatre in the Age of Irving*. Totawa: Rowman and Littlefield, 1981.

_____. *The Victorian Theatre*. 2nd ed. Cambridge: Cambridge University Press, 1978.

The Royal Shakespeare Theatre. *Pictures and Sculptures from the Royal Shakespeare Theatre Picture Gallery*. Stratford-upon-Avon: The Royal Shakespeare Theatre Picture Gallery and Museum, 1961.

Salaman, Malcom C. *Shakespeare in Pictorial Art*. London: The Studio, 1916.

Schoenbaum, Samuel. *Shakespeare, the Globe and the World*. New York: The Folger Shakespeare Library and Oxford University Press, 1979.

Sprague, Arthur Colby. *Shakespearean Players and Performances*. Cambridge, Mass: Harvard University Press, 1953.

Stokes, John. *Resistible Theatres: Enterprise and Experiment in the Late Nineteenth Century*. London: Paul Elek Books, Ltd., 1972.

Strong, Roy C. *Recreating the Past: British History and the Victorian Painter.* New York: Thames and Hudson, 1978.

Styan, J. L. *The Shakespeare Revolution: Criticism and Performances in the Twentieth Century.* Cambridge: Cambridge University Press, 1977.

Sund, Judy. "Benjamin West: A Scene from *King Lear*." *Bulletin of the Detroit Institute of Arts* 58 (1980): 127-36.

Williams, Gary J. "Madame Vestris' *A Midsummer Night's Dream* and the Web of Victorian Tradition." *Theatre Survey* 18 (1979): 1-22.

PHOTOGRAPHY CREDITS

(Figure numbers preceded by "0" refer to illustrations in "Words into Pictures: Shakespeare in British Art 1760-1902" by Lucy Oakley, those preceded by "M" refer to illustrations in "The Theatre of Illusion" by Cary Mazer.)

Ackland Art Museum, University of North Carolina at Chapel Hill, Photographic Services, *Chapel Hill, North Carolina,* cat. no. 12.

Katherine Baetjer, *New York, New York,* fig. 024.

City of Birmingham Museum and Art Gallery, Photographic Services, *Birmingham England,* fig. 020.

Boston Museum of Fine Arts, Department of Photographic Services, *Boston, Massachusetts,* fig. 08.

The University of Bristol Theatre Collection, The Beerbohem Tree Collection, *Bristol, England,* fig. M8.

Carlisle Museum and Art Gallery, *Carlisle England,* cat. no. 57.

Carnegie Institute, Museum of Arts, Photographic Services, *Pittsburgh, Pennsylvania,* cat. no. 2.

Judy Cooper, Kurt Schon, Ltd., *New Orleans, Louisiana,* cat. nos. 6, 7, 8, 9, 10, 11, 13, 15, 16, 19, 20, 21, 23, 26, 27, 32, 33, 35, 40, 41, 43, 44, 48, 50, 54, 58, 62.

The Corcoran Gallery of Art, Photographic Services, *Washington, D.C.,* cat. no. 38.

Courtauld Institute of Art, Christopher Gatiss Photographic Survey, *London, England,* fig. 018.

George M. Cushing, Photography, *Boston, Massachusetts,* cat. no. 5.

E. T. Archives, *London, England,* cat. no. 18.

The Folger Shakespeare Library, Photographic Services, *Washington, D.C.,* cat. nos. 25, 53, 55, 56, 61, figs. 07, 09, 016.

The FORBES Magazine Collection, *New York, New York,* cat. nos. 17, 34, 51, 52.

Furness Memorial Library, Van Pelt Library, *University of Pennsylvania,* Philadelphia, Pennsylvania, figs. M4, M5.

Godfrey New Photographics Ltd., *Kent, England,* fig. 011.

Harvard Theatre Collection, Harvard Collection Library, *Cambridge, Massachusetts,* figs. M2, M7.

Kunsthaus Photographic Services, *Zurich, Switzerland,* fig. 04.

Kunstmuseum, Photographic Services, *Winterthur, Switzerland,* fig. 06.

Paulus Leeser, *Poughkeepsie, New York,* cat. no. 28.

Leighton House Museum and Art Gallery, Photographic Services, *London, England,* cat. no. 36.

Cary Mazer, *Philadelphia, Pennsylvania,* fig. M6.

John Mills (Photography, Ltd.) *Liverpool, England,* fig. 01.

The Honorable Francis D. Murnaghan, Jr., *Baltimore, Maryland,* cat. no. 45.

Museo de Arte de Ponce, *Ponce, Puerto Rico,* cat. no. 49.

Peter Nahum, *London, England,* cat. no. 14.

National Galleries of Scotland, Photographic Services, *Edinburgh, Scotland,* fig. 03.

National Portrait Gallery, Photographic Services, *Washington, D.C.,* cat. no. 31.

National Theatre Press Office, *London, England,* cat. no. 64.

New Orleans Museum of Art, Photographic Services, *New Orleans, Louisiana,* cat. no. 63.

The Pennsylvania Academy of the Fine Arts, Photographic Services, *Philadelphia, Pennsylvania,* cat. no. 60, fig. 013.

The Players, Hampton-Booth Theatre Library, *New York, New York,* fig. M9.

Regis Corporation, *Minneapolis, Minnesota,* fig. 015.

Rodney Todd—White and Son Photographers, *London, England,* fig. 02.

Edwin S. Roseberry, University of Virginia, Photographic Services, *Charlottesville, Virginia,* cat. no. 47.

Royal Academy of Arts, Photo Studios Ltd., *London, England,* cat. nos. 22, 37.

Tom Scott, *Edinburgh, Scotland,* fig. 017.

Studio Nine, Inc., *New York, New York,* cat. no. 46.

Joseph Szaszfai, *Branford, Connecticut,* cat. nos. 1, 3, 4, 42, fig. 022.

The Tate Gallery, Photographic Services, *London, England,* figs. 019, 021.

Unusual Films, *Greenville, South Carolina,* cat. nos. 29, 30, 39, 59.

Van Pelt Library, Special Collections, *Philadelphia, Pennsylvania,* fig. M1.

Wallace Collection, Photographic Services, *London, England,* fig. 012.

Herbert P. Vose, *Chatham, Massachusetts,* cat. no. 24.

Yale Center for British Art, Photographic Services, *New Haven, Connecticut,* figs. 010, 014, 023.